DOMINIQUE ANSEL

SECRET RECIPES
FROM THE WORLD FAMOUS
NEW YORK BAKERY

FOREWORD BY
DANIEL BOULUD

PHOTOGRAPHS BY
THOMAS SCHAUER

MURDOCH BOOKS

Published in 2015 by Murdoch Books, an imprint of Allen & Unwin
First published by Simon & Schuster in 2014

Murdoch Books Australia
83 Alexander Street
Crows Nest NSW 2065
Phone: +61 (0) 2 8425 0100
www.murdochbooks.com.au
info@murdochbooks.com.au

Murdoch Books UK
Ormond House, 26-27 Boswell Street,
London WC1N 3JZ
Phone: +44 (0) 20 8785 5995
www.murdochbooks.co.uk
info@murdochbooks.co.uk

For corporate orders & custom publishing contact our
business development team at salesenquiries@murdochbooks.com.au

Interior design by Suet Yee Chong
Jacket design by Marilyn Dantes
Photography by Thomas Schauer

A cataloguing-in-publication entry is available from the catalogue of the National Library of Australia at www.nla.gov.au.

ISBN 978 1 74336 577 9 Australia
ISBN 978 1 74336 578 6 UK

A catalogue record for this book is available from the British Library.

Printed in China by C&C Offset Printing Co., Ltd.
10 9 8 7 6 5

IMPORTANT: Those who might be at risk from the effects of salmonella poisoning (the elderly, pregnant women, young children
and those suffering from immune deficiency diseases) should consult their doctor with any concerns about eating raw eggs.

OVEN GUIDE: You may find cooking times vary depending on the oven you are using. For fan-forced ovens, as a general rule,
set the oven temperature to 70°F (20°C) lower than indicated in the recipe.

MEASURES GUIDE: The recipes in this book use 15 ml (3 teaspoon) tablespoon measures.

NOTES ON INGREDIENTS:
Fleur de sel is a type of sea salt. Regular sea salt can be used in its place.
Kosher salt is preferred in these recipes for its flaky consistency. If Kosher salt is unavailable, use an equal amount of sea salt
or ¾ teaspoon of table salt for each 1 teaspoon of Kosher salt asked for.
Pearl sugar consists of extra large sugar crystals and is used for finishing and decoration.
Plain lour is also sometimes called all-purpose flour.
Pouring cream is also sometimes called thin or pure cream, among other names. The key to identifying the correct cream is
its fat content — look for a fat content around 35% for this kind of cream.
Unsweetened cocoa paste, also called cacao paste or mass, is pure bitter chocolate.

TO A.
FROM A CASE OF CHERRIES
TO A LIFE OF CHEERING,
YOU INSPIRE ME EVERY DAY.
D.

CONTENTS

FOREWORD

I am proud to contribute to Dominique's first book, not only as a former employer and longtime friend, but, more important, because I like to think we both share a special kinship as dreamers. Great chefs don't ask "Why?" They ask "Why not?" They aren't afraid of a challenge and they aren't afraid to break the rules. But they also have the technical training necessary to play with recipes while intuitively knowing which crucial steps should not be sacrificed. Dominique has demonstrated—and will continue to demonstrate—these exceptional qualities.

While he was the pastry chef at Daniel, Dominique challenged us to experiment more. He often tapped into our savoury pantry or looked to other cultures for inspiration. He was the first to introduce to the pastry menu elements like basil seeds, olive oil powder, *horchata* ice cream, and *shiso* sorbet. His talent was in reaching afar for something exciting and then working until it made sense within our determinedly French menu.

He approached classic American flavours with the naive curiosity of a student in his first cooking class. Why do the combinations of peanut butter and chocolate—or Key lime and graham cracker—get people so excited?

However, he also respected certain recipes and kept them as they were. Our magical madeleine, for example: that simply cannot change, because it has become so iconic to our customers, who have committed its taste and texture to memory.

I remember when Dominique was ready to branch out on his own. As a chef-owner, I always focus on our own program, but I strongly support the talent of my team members. I was happy to see that he could make his dreams come true on his own. Like all of our former pastry chefs, he has left an imprint that will be remembered.

When Dominique opened his pastry shop in SoHo, he jumped from managing a ten-item pastry menu with one service to an all-day menu consisting of *viennoiseries*, pastries, desserts, cookies, candies, sandwiches and more. His passion for constant improvement is palpable, whether it's on the classics that he has practised since his very first job in Paris, or on the creations he discovered while on his global travels. I am pleased that Dominique has continued to represent the DNA of French patisserie while embracing a true New York *je ne sais quoi*. Items on his menu such as the Paris–New York, which has the texture of a Paris-Brest and the taste of a Snickers bar, is a great example of a hybrid from his imagination.

I had no doubt that he would excel and become the sensation that he is today, although perhaps not even I could have anticipated the media frenzy that ensued over the Cronut™ pastry! As long as I can have a seat on his cozy patio to enjoy his latest creation with an espresso, I'll be happy. I hope that as you read this book, you will be inspired to create not just the recipes within, but also to think creatively in your own day-to-day baking adventures, just as Dominique would have you do.

—DANIEL BOULUD,
CHEF-OWNER, RESTAURANT DANIEL, NEW YORK CITY

INTRODUCTION

I was thirty-four years old when I opened my own bakery, but by then I had already been working in a kitchen for more than half my life. I first walked into a professional kitchen at the age of sixteen, and I don't think I can imagine a day when I would ever leave. I was taught to cook the old-fashioned way. Within the ranks of the French kitchen brigade, your job was simple:

1. Look closely at what your chef is doing.
2. Copy it as exactly as you can.
3. Repeat hundreds of times.

It felt like tracing the letters of someone else's handwriting, until you no longer remembered your own. And while this method trains highly proficient cooks, it doesn't nurture innovators.

Something's wrong with the system. Cooks should be taught not only how to replicate, but also how to *innovate*. Learning how to perform a set task is certainly easier than finding a whole new way to interpret it. Inspiration can't be measured on a scale. Passion can't be chopped up on a cutting board or added to a recipe—like seasoning—at will. But all these factors must be present to produce something truly ground-breaking.

People often ask me if I keep my recipes under lock and key. On the contrary, they are printed out and kept in a blue folder in the kitchen for all to access. Recipes are just pieces of paper. No ratio of ingredients or list of instructions could ever be the key to success. The real secrets are hidden in the stories behind each creation. And that's what I will share with you in this book.

This is the way I teach the young pastry chefs who come through my kitchen how to not just cook, but how to create.

I have divided this book into two sections. In the first, I reveal what I've learned as I crafted some of my favourite pastries. These lessons can be applied to all areas of life. A bite-size cake can teach you about the preciousness of time. A tart can show you how to dream. A scoop of ice cream can renew your appreciation of simplicity. The second half of the book holds the recipes to some of my most sought-after creations. This is where you have a chance to get your hands dirty, so you can follow my footsteps in your kitchen. And my hope is that someday you will go on to explore new ground of your own.

Happy baking, eating, and—most of all—creating!

Dominique Ansel

1

TIME IS AN INGREDIENT

We eat thousands of meals in our lifetimes, but just a fraction of them are impactful enough to endure in our memory. And sometimes eating, much like breathing, becomes nothing more than a secondary action. Repetition of any action dulls the senses over time, but imagine if you could hit reset and treat each moment as the first. Even the most ordinary things can unlock the most profound inspirations.

For me, my first *real* memory of food is a simple one: the warmth of the baguette between my legs as my dad drove home from the neighbourhood bakery; the smell of the yeast filling the car; the crinkle of the wax paper bag; and the crunch of the crust as I wrestled off piece after piece, starting from the heel, and devoured them with delight. That baguette did not survive long enough to make it to the family dining table. The vividness of this memory lingers in my mind like a scene from a dream.

Just what about this baguette—from a no-name bakery, made by the hands of an unknown baker—made it stand out from all the other more extravagant meals I've had? I struggled to find the answer for years, and then realised it was all about timing. So much of food and good cooking is just that: paying attention to the invisible yet indispensable ingredient of *time*. Just as every flower blooms until its peak right before the blossom wilts, all foods—in fact, all creations—have that perfect moment as well. And when the timing is right, a simple thing can become transformative. Pure and immaculate, it can nourish not only the senses, but also the soul.

Preparing a great pastry is always a rush or a wait for that perfect moment.

Every crusty, custardy, sweet cannelé resists the shortcuts cooks try to use in making them. There is no cheating when it comes to a cannelé, and in these pages you'll learn why. I'll talk about madeleines and how they're similar to cherry blossoms in the beauty and the brevity of their shelf life. Just five minutes out of the oven, and they are a completely different product. The opposite holds true for the macaron, and I explain why it's one of the items *not* meant to be eaten fresh. Finally, I share my story of why I've never had a decent chocolate chip cookie in France, and why I think moments in time have everything to do with that.

We live in a world where every creation strives to be both instantaneous and eternal. To respect time as the supreme ingredient is a battle of breaking habits and changing perceptions. Nobody likes to wait; nobody likes to rush. But when you treat time as an ingredient, it changes everything.

There is always the temptation to 'cheat'. In school on a test, at work on a project, and in the kitchen. We all want to fast-forward to the good parts.

So you start to think of what you can do without. You don't *have* to gently stir milk with a wooden spoon as it boils; leaving it there pretty much does the trick. And while eggs work well in certain recipes at room temperature, you don't want to wait hours for them to get there. When I first entered my culinary training, an instructor told me, 'Taking shortcuts is not cheating. It's getting to the *same* destination, but faster.' That year, I discovered new techniques, improved my efficiency, and found faster methods to make almost everything . . . until I tried my hand at the cannelé.

A pastry from Bordeaux, the cannelé is not much for looks. On the outside, there's a dark, hard shell that can be mistaken for burnt. But for those who bite into the crunchy exterior, there is the illuminating reward of a tender, flan-like core, rich with the scent of vanilla and rum. To achieve those delicately balanced results, there is only one road, and no shortcuts. The cannelé demands your time; it magnifies your mistakes.

The first decision to make is what type of mould to purchase. The traditional copper moulds from which the cannelé gets its signature shape are small, cylindrical and striated. They must first be seasoned by brushing melted beeswax in the interior and heating each mould in the oven four or five times, until the metal pores have absorbed the wax, a process you'll need to repeat one or two times after every wash to prevent your batter from sticking. If you try an easier option, like a nonstick silicone mould, you will lose that crunchy, caramelised exterior, and instead the result will be spongy and soft. Don't do it—stay the course.

When it comes to the point of making the batter—a relatively simple recipe similar to that for a crêpe—you must mix slowly. Rush the process and you'll end up with large bubbles in your custard instead of the small, effervescent ones you should be achieving for that perfect texture. And what awaits you around the bend is another endurance test: a twenty-four-hour wait for the gluten in the batter to rest, ensuring that your cannelé rises straight up in the mould when you bake it. Try to cheat the system and you'll get a misshapen cannelé full of holes.

You aren't even done when you put the cannelé in the oven. The baking tray on which the mould rests needs to be rotated every fifteen minutes or so as the cannelé bakes. Even now, so close to the finish line, the product will sink like a soufflé without careful attention.

A cannelé isn't just a pastry; it is proof of the cook's patience and dedication. Some creations demand everything you have and don't dignify anything less than your best efforts with the perfect outcome. We have all been tempted by an easier path. Perhaps no one saw the places where we cut the corners, or caught us brushing certain things under the rug. But that's the difference between those pieces of work and a masterpiece. The same lesson applies to the most challenging tasks down to a simple meal. My advice would be to skip the flashy dinner for two the next time you want to show you care—nothing says 'I love you' like a single perfect cannelé.

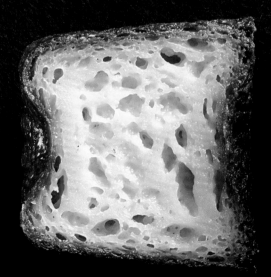

THE BRIEF LIFE OF THE MADELEINE

Stop thinking of a dessert as just an object, and start seeing it as a living thing. And then, try to really believe it.

The way I see it, the first time ingredients touch my hands, it sets off a spark of life that runs through the dish I'm working on. If the Sistine Chapel were reinterpreted by the mind of a cook, God would be wearing a toque and his finger would be reaching out for a kitchen tool. We've all felt it—there's an inherent energy of life behind every dish. Leftover casseroles deepen in character. Herbs wilt, then blossom when they hit the hot surface of meat, unlocking their inner fragrance. A carton of ice cream sitting at room temperature starts to soften and temper as if awakening from hibernation. Food changes and grows; it lives and then it also dies. And for the fleeting and forever young madeleine, death comes all too soon.

Fresh out of the oven, these small, scallop-shaped cakes shine in a momentary glory. A slightly crispy edge gives way to a golden, ethereal centre that releases just a tiny puff of steam in your mouth, as if exhaling its last breath.

But just five minutes after your introduction, everything starts to change. The once-pillowy bites become as dense as pebbles. The crispy edges turn sticky and stale. And the light dusting of icing sugar fades into a greyish hue as it soaks into the crumb. Dull and lacklustre, the late madeleine sits in front of you hardened and dry—the very embodiment of what a pastry corpse would look like. Blink and you'll miss it at its best.

Just one experience of the short and precious life of the madeleine should teach you that it's not only about the cooking, but also about the eating. When you make something to be enjoyed, the creation is just as much about the person on the receiving end as the one who produced it. The madeleine demands that both chef and taster stop their plans, stand by the oven, and wait. It reminds me of the time I woke up to see the sunrise. Stumbling around in the darkness and staring at the violet-blue twilight for long, sleepy moments until those gratifying few minutes when the sun peeked out from the horizon. It's one of nature's best artworks and cannot be captured by any museum. The only option is to wait.

This is easier said than done. Everyone understands the general logic of a 'life span' for food, but when you ask them to really believe, to respect it, and to wait, it becomes a different story. We all have plans; we all need to be somewhere. And sometimes it seems easy to buy a prepackaged madeleine rich with greasy butter that helps keep it alive for longer and all but wipes out its true nature.

I make my madeleines to order. I don't pipe them or bake them until someone is standing there waiting for them. And as they stand there, rushed and frustrated at having to compromise their life and their schedule for a pastry, they often ask me why they should bother waiting.

'Quite simply,' I answer, 'it is a matter of life and death.'

'FOOD CHANGES AND GROWS;
IT LIVES AND THEN IT ALSO DIES.
AND FOR THE FLEETING AND
FOREVER YOUNG MADELEINE,
DEATH COMES ALL TOO SOON.'

No one paid much attention to the three old cooks at Fauchon, my alma mater and the place where I 'graduated' to become a working pastry cook. Some couldn't tell them apart: each one sported the same bushy moustache, round belly, and greying hair. Decades ago they were young boys, as I was when I first entered the kitchens of this pastry institution. But now in their fifties, they had lost their youthful competitiveness and quietly faded into the background like the walls or shelves. These men were my secret weapon.

Whenever I came across a problem I couldn't solve, one of them seemed to have the answer. They couldn't explain their reasoning in words, but their hands knew the way to manipulate ingredients until they obeyed. One of them, Didier, had the sole task of making macarons. These French almond meringue cookies consumed ten to twelve hours of his day as he mixed the batter, then piped and filled hundreds of them in the basement kitchen of the Fauchon flagship on the Place de la Madeleine in Paris.

Upstairs in the brightly lit shop, perfumed ladies giggled as they pointed their manicured fingers at his jewel-like work, the colours as vivid as their lipsticks. That first bite was always an experience: a gossamer-thin shell that crunched slightly with the gentle pressure of your teeth, which then sank into a moist, tender centre with a vibrant burst of flavour. 'Fresh handmade macarons are the latest treat,' one lady gushed with delight.

And she was correct on all but one point. You see, well-made macarons are not actually 'fresh'. Just out of the oven, the macaron shells are in fact dry and brittle on the edges. And while most pastries are at their best fresh and just baked, the macaron is a counterexample.

The process of making a proper macaron involves a crucial step in which it must sit in the refrigerator for at least a day to absorb the humidity from the surrounding air as well as moisture from the filling. It's this tempering process that rehydrates and revives it to give a great macaron its incomparable texture. In a sense, a macaron must 'live a little' and come into its full character with time.

The macaron is a late developer in a world obsessed with freshness as the ideal. But like the cook whose hands probably touched every well-loved Fauchon macaron in Paris for decades, *older* doesn't necessarily mean *lesser.*

Years later, Fauchon moved its production operations to a larger facility away from the store. Didier moved with it. The company invested money into a high-speed macaron-piping machine, which he learned to operate. But I swear that Didier could pipe just as fast or even faster by hand. On his own, he produced more than two or three times the number of macarons than did men half his age, and his tenure at Fauchon impressively outlasted many of its greatest pastry chefs. It didn't always come easy for Didier, I'm sure. But with time came mastery.

When I rose up the ranks far enough to manage my own team at Fauchon, I saw the young apprentices beneath me panic in frustration when their hands hadn't developed the dexterity to do what they were instructed. The quality of their initial work was something Didier would've frowned upon, but it was also the story of Didier that became the motivation to keep them trying.

'A MACARON MUST "LIVE A LITTLE"
AND COME INTO ITS
FULL CHARACTER WITH TIME.'

MEMORIES WITHIN A COOKIE

The newspaper headline caught my eye: AMERICA'S FAVOURITE DESSERT IS THE COOKIE. Below, a paragraph reported that seven out of ten Americans chose the cookie as their favourite baked good, with 10 per cent claiming they ate a cookie every single day. Sitting there in my tiny apartment in France at the age of twenty-five, I was baffled by these statistics. I had never been to America, and I had yet to taste a cookie I actually liked.

When I was growing up, cookies were one of the least popular items in my neighbourhood bakery. Children would much prefer a croissant or an éclair over any cookie, which sat on the back shelves and dried out as the day passed. Yet somehow, an ocean away, there was an entire nation that shared a genuine and unanimous love for this one triumphant product. No single pastry in France unites the people in the same way.

The first time I ever visited the United States, I tried every cookie I could find in the stores. They didn't taste *that* different from the ones in France, I thought. Nothing exotic or out of the ordinary. But I watched the eyes of locals light up with passion when asked the simple question: What's your favourite cookie?

Their answers were always different. Thick or thin, crispy or chewy, with or without nuts—everyone defended their choices vehemently. Some liked chocolate chip, some preferred oatmeal raisin. I learned what a snickerdoodle was. Everyone agreed they loved cookies, but disagreed on what made a good cookie. 'I make my cookies with milk and dark chocolate chips,' one person told me. 'Use brown sugar,' came another tip. 'I like to use molasses for mine,' someone added.

And then—a breakthrough. I realised everyone was speaking to me from the perspective of a cook, not a customer. The cookies in their minds weren't the ones they purchased, but the ones they made themselves.

For many of these people, cookies were the very first thing they baked as children. They remembered emptying the chocolate chips into the bowl, rolling small balls of dough, and watching them spread and bake in the oven. It was an after-school pastime or a weekend activity. It was for a loved one as a gift, or a tradition during the holidays. And everyone pinpointed as the greatest satisfaction that final reveal from the oven, when they could bite into a warm, just-baked cookie. These people were no longer merely tasting the flavours; they were tasting a moment in time.

Time is not simply a measurement of minutes and hours, but also a keeper of experiences. Even people who have very different tastes feel united by the roles that food plays in their lives. And truly great creations transport us to another time by making a connection that transcends the present. The cookie is the ultimate time traveller.

The first time I actually enjoyed a cookie was when I made it myself from scratch with my sous chef in the kitchens of the New York restaurant Daniel during my first few years there. She, of course, had made it many times growing up in the United States. It was late at night and we had just finished an especially tough day. We poured chocolate chips into a bowl, we rolled the dough into round balls and flattened them slightly, and then we waited by the oven for them to bake. The ones that we made were chocolaty, flourless, slightly crispy on the edges like the corner piece of a brownie, and extra moist, almost cake-like in the centre. It was the first cookie that was mine.

Today, that's the type of cookie I make. It's a recipe that you might want to alter and adapt to your own tastes. But it's what I consider to be the best cookie, for the same reasons everyone else has their own favourites. And we're all absolutely right.

'TRULY GREAT CREATIONS TRANSPORT
US TO ANOTHER TIME BY MAKING A CONNECTION
THAT TRANSCENDS THE PRESENT. THE COOKIE
IS THE ULTIMATE TIME TRAVELLER.'

2

BEYOND THE COMFORT ZONE

Firsts are always uncomfortable. A first taste, a first look, a first attempt—despite the promise of something new just beyond—each is approached with a pause and then an uncertain first step. And for many of us, no 'first' causes more anxiety than the first day of work.

There are two first days I'll always remember: 1 September 1999 was my first day of work at Fauchon. I'll never forget stumbling through the legendary Parisian pastry house's maze of hallways and doors until I found the production kitchen.

Eight years later, I walked into the restaurant Daniel in New York with the same uncertain footsteps.

It's amazing how similar the two days were. In both cases, I was immediately handed my uniform. At Fauchon it was the signature black cotton with hot-pink stitching, which I wore along with a group of eager guys who were all competing for just one full-time position. At Daniel, it was white, crisply ironed, and had my name stitched onto the pocket in golden-bronze thread. And despite the years that separated my first days in Paris with those in New York, where I entered as the executive pastry chef, I still felt like a fish out of water.

I wasn't worried about my technical skills or ability to manage a kitchen team, but I quickly realised that New York worked by a different set of rules. Here, the chef was no longer king; instead, every customer who came in the door held a higher sovereignty. Substitutions, special requests and accommodations were not the exception here but the norm. Over the next six years at Daniel, I learned one important lesson: a truly appreciated creation isn't made for the creator, but for the audience to enjoy.

This chapter is about my trek beyond my comfort zone. I confess my hatred of working with meringue but share how confronting the pavlova taught me to find joy in great obstacles. One particular chocolate creation redefined my concept of beauty and destruction, and I tell that story, too. I talk about how my journey to make marshmallow chicks revealed the difficulties of picking up a new tradition and of bridging the gap between what may seem incompatible at first glance. And finally, I explore the territory of creating food that must travel and how I overcame it with my own mix of cereal.

Creativity requires effort. It is always a strain, a leap beyond the periphery of comfort. With these new recipes, be prepared to feel as I did—uncomfortable. Pastry is not an intuitive study; when you haven't worked with similar tools in the same steps, there's a natural clumsiness. But when the day arrives that you feel completely at ease with the recipes within these pages, promise me that you will move on to another book, and in that process become an even better cook.

By the end of January 2000, I managed to beat out twenty or so other cooks for one highly coveted position at Fauchon. Later, I figured that if I could do that, I would be up for the challenge that awaited me in the States, where I would oversee the dessert menu at Daniel, having at the time never created a plated dessert for a restaurant—a very different skill set from bakery desserts—in my life. At my formal inauguration, chef Daniel Boulud stood next to me at the manager's meeting and introduced me to the entire team. 'Dominique,' he said, 'welcome to America.' It was a new job, a new country, and a newer world than I had ever imagined I'd experience. But that's the whole point now, isn't it?

THE PAVLOVA WEAK SPOT

Here is a secret: I hate meringues.

Something about the crunch as they crumble under the pressure of my fork is like nails screeching across a chalkboard. Their fragile, light-as-air demeanour, which is always threatening to crack, has been my culinary kryptonite. Every hair on my forearms stands up in absolute rejection of these dried-out sugared egg whites.

I can't explain why. But I firmly believe that anyone who walks far enough down the avenues of their craft eventually stumbles upon their strengths as well as their weaknesses. There are harmonies and discords, loves and hates. You have to start cooking to discover them.

Cold hands make working with dough a smoother process, allowing you to line your tart shells or laminate croissants with ease, without melting the butter or fat within. Dexterous fingers are perfect for adding those final flourishes of fruit and décor to a pastry. And sensitive skin can detect temperatures of cooling chocolate with more precision during the tempering process. Everyone has their own knack that reveals itself in the beginning stages of their learning process. It's the things that go against our natural faculties that can block our ability to be true creators. When you find out what those are for you, the first step is to confess.

Without realising it, I had always refrained from serving meringues on my menus. Compared to mousses or ice creams, it wasn't the most popular item and so years passed before I paid much attention to it. That is, until the gluten-free revolution. With so many customers cutting wheat from their diet, meringue had the potential to become a key player in the pastry world. And one summer, I experienced a deluge of requests for the pavlova, a simple dessert composed from a trifecta of ingredients: fruit, cream and meringue.

A gorgeous pavlova is a subtle play of texture. As the moisture from the cream soaks into the meringue, it adds a slight chewiness to its core and accentuates the crispiness of its shell. It took weeks to calibrate that perfect meringue shell, at times hollowing out the centre for an even more delicate product. Every day of that summer, I handmade and assembled hundreds of pavlovas, and every time a powdery shell scraped against the surface of another, shivers ran down my spine. The process battered and bruised my senses—and funny enough, it never got better. I hate working with meringue to this day. But a good fight is never an easy one.

The pavlova became an item that I would regularly keep on my menu. The name of my very first pavlova was the Black and Blue. Casual observers assume its moniker is derived from the blackberries encased inside the blueberry meringue. But in truth, I was inspired by the beating that I took to finish it. I named it after the struggle: taking punches, and standing back up.

INSPIRED BY A PEEP

There's a game I've been playing for years: I'll name a specific holiday and ask someone to say the first ingredient that comes to mind. It's incredible how there's almost a Pavlovian link between special occasions and food. Before long, people begin to describe entire menus. Christmas is almost always cinnamon, a warm spice that morphs into imaginary gingerbread, cookies and pies. New Year's? I can bet you it's Champagne, perhaps infused into macerated ripe strawberries. And Easter, for as long as I remembered, was chocolate.

Growing up in France, I remember the shelves of local chocolatiers stacked with chocolate eggs every Easter. It is a memory that I

thought every kid shared. But when I asked Americans to describe their Easter memories, rather than chocolate eggs, they talked instead about marshmallows. Hearing an unexpected answer so many times made me realise that maybe *I* was the outlier, not everyone else.

I soon discovered some Americans are loyal to traditional chocolate eggs, but an equally strong contingent will choose marshmallow chicks. Deciding between the two is as futile as the age-old question of the chicken or the egg. Neither of them can win over the other.

Could I create a marshmallow chick similar to the multiple ones out there in the market? Of course. Making a new pastry with a

different medium isn't technically difficult, and I enjoyed working with marshmallow. But to diverge from the deep and powerful memories of my childhood, and to do it with a bit of wit and cleverness—that's like trying to make a joke in a foreign language.

More than six years passed between the first time I tried a Peep, the best-known brand of marshmallow chicks, and the first time I attempted my own version. I used cleaned eggshells with their tops precisely severed. A double dollop of marshmallow on the top transformed the eggshells into the homes of small chicks. They were dusted in the same familiar yellow sugar and brought to life with tiny black chocolate dots as eyes, through which they peered out innocently. In this creation, I combined the egg and marshmallow—it was my way of keeping a little bit of the Easter I celebrated in my childhood.

Did I really need that length of time to do something with marshmallow chicks for Easter? No. But there's sincerity in adopting a tradition first, rather than forcing a solution. I had received so many marshmallow chicks as presents from my American staff that by the time the holiday rolled around, I had gotten used to expecting them.

There's never a rush to create. Take some time to truly immerse yourself, and the genuine thoughts that come out—as simple as they may be—will shine through.

'SOME AMERICANS ARE LOYAL TO TRADITIONAL
CHOCOLATE EGGS, BUT AN EQUALLY STRONG CONTINGENT
WILL CHOOSE MARSHMALLOW CHICKS.
DECIDING BETWEEN THE TWO IS AS FUTILE AS THE
AGE-OLD QUESTION OF THE CHICKEN OR THE EGG.'

CRACKING THE CHOCOLATE EGG

'It's too beautiful to eat,' said the customer, intending it as a compliment. I didn't know quite how to take it. But something in my gut felt the thud of disappointment.

I had made hundreds of chocolate Easter eggs that year. Each was a laboured process. It took three hours to craft not just one but three eggs of increasing size, which were nestled together like a set of Russian matryoshka dolls. The outermost layer was a dark chocolate shell, dusted in gold, with strategically punctured holes that allowed you to peer inside. There you would find a white chocolate shell shining out in sharp contrast. And within that, a milk chocolate egg that held three types of chocolate truffles.

The truffles were Champagne-, orange- and pistachio-flavoured. But most of the customers never got around to tasting any of them. Instead, their chocolate eggs sat around through the summer months until they became dull and too old to eat and were tossed out like a still-wrapped present. Being 'too beautiful' was a curse that prevented these chocolate Easter eggs from fulfilling their destiny—to be sloppily and uninhibitedly consumed with delight.

This wasn't a problem I had encountered before, back home in France. Lavish gilded Easter eggs were standard there, and customers didn't hesitate to unwrap them and break their shells. But such Fabergé-inspired creations didn't have the same effect in New York.

Here, beauty was a deterrent to destruction. And the act of eating requires that something be broken to be devoured. It's triumphant and messy, and you wipe your mouth at the end of it.

How would I create something 'ugly' enough to be eaten?

Clearly, I didn't want to compromise on the quality of presentation. As the months passed and seasons changed, I wondered what I would design next Easter. One day, I delivered a cake to a child's birthday party, where a piñata hung in the cleared centre of a restaurant's private room. The young guests laughed mischievously as they swung the bat. A lightbulb went on. This was the type of reaction I wanted to harness. Not the subtle eyebrow raises and the whispered comments of an art museum.

When Easter rolled around, I was ready. I unveiled an all-red egg with menacing eyebrows and a sharp beak. It was inspired by the popular video game Angry Birds, where the only objective is to launch birds with a slingshot and destroy structures. This chocolate egg was daring you to break it. And it captured the joy of destruction.

Inside I generously stuffed bonbons, caramels and marshmallows. This was the reward, the conquest, the level-up. Every single chocolate egg was broken that year, just as all great culinary creations should be.

SAVING CEREAL FOR CHRISTMAS

There's a problem that pastry chefs throughout history have struggled to solve. How can delicate desserts be transported across great distances, especially when most of them can barely survive a New York City subway ride?

Across the globe, chefs have tried to manage the situation with various manoeuvres. I was once denied the right to buy a cake in Tokyo because I confessed I was staying at a hotel that was located more than fifteen minutes away. Some shops package their goods with pages of instructions that will probably be tossed in the trash along with the bag. Others have employees repeat long speeches on the best storage recommendations as they stuff ice packs into the box. Nothing works perfectly.

At a restaurant, the chef determines how each dish arrives, and each plate is cleared before the next one is served. But in a shop, you hand over your creations and what happens next is beyond your control. You can't force people to stay in one place. Damage is inevitable.

The only solution, I realised, would be to stop thinking about this as a problem and embrace it as an opportunity. I wanted to create something that actually does travel well. And what time do people travel the most? Christmas. In this season of gifting and family reunions, nobody wants to go back home empty-handed.

But packaged products often don't have the same alluring appeal as a fresh dessert. Perhaps you remember a time when you received a Christmas goodie bag and unexcitedly nibbled from it until spring. I wanted an item that would survive the trip and be ready to share with everyone once it landed. How can you get someone to rip open the package and eat immediately?

I didn't realise that I was looking at the answer every morning. In those sleepy early hours, the one item I always reach out for, almost by reflex, is the cereal box. Cereal is a part of everyday life: you're not saving it for a special occasion; you want it for its convenience and satisfaction regularly.

I went to work and coated puffed rice cereal in caramelised milk chocolate and tossed it with smoked-cinnamon meringues and caramelised hazelnuts. It's what I would've liked waking up to early on Christmas morning as a child, then spending the rest of the day in pyjamas opening up presents.

Christmas Morning Cereal was an experiment that quickly grew to one of our most popular holiday specialties. Hundreds of boxes went out that year, hand-carried by loved ones to places as distant as Asia and Australia. And my hope is that on Christmas morning it made everyone's breakfast a little sweeter.

3

DON'T LISTEN

My parents tell me that the first word I ever said was 'yes'. Of course, I may have been trying to say something else, since I was sputtering all sorts of unformed noises at the time. But I like to think it is true, and I often wonder what it was that inspired me to break my silence.

I live by the rule that if you don't have anything worthwhile to say, you shouldn't speak at all. But perhaps one of the quietest times of my life took place when I first started my own bakery.

It took just seven of the most backbreaking, sweat-drenching and utterly frustrating weeks from the time I left my previous job at Daniel until the opening day. During that entire period, despite the fact that I was trying to build my vision, I was silent. Something within me withdrew into the solitude of my infant days.

As it turned out, it was a lot easier to not *speak* than it was to not *listen*. Everyone else had something to say about my next step.

'You should focus on selling sandwiches,' one person suggested. 'People don't buy pastries these days. They'll buy sandwiches during lunchtime. That's where you make the money.'

'You should make cupcakes,' another recommended. 'It's New York! People love cupcakes.'

'Lower the prices,' said one.

'Increase the prices,' suggested another.

There I found myself, at the beginning of the next stage of my career, and I could barely hear my own thoughts above the chatter of everyone else's. I understood that their advice was well intentioned, but I knew I had to decide the way forward for myself. I needed to learn how to *not* listen.

The world speaks only to what has already happened: tales of those who have already succeeded, those who have already failed. Advice is based on history rather than possibility. And only when you stop listening do you stop imitating and start creating. In this chapter, I'll take you through decisions I made that at first may seem counterintuitive, like launching a pastry called the DKA, which everyone told me would never catch on. I'll describe rule-breaking stunts like the Magic Soufflé, and I'll share the story behind the infamous Cronut™ pastry. I'll end with a caveat: it's also important to remember that some things require no change at all, as is the case with vanilla ice cream.

Take a moment with me and try to not listen. Dig within yourself to find the things you deeply care about and believe in. And when you hit upon what inspires you most, the doubt will dissipate. The right path will be clear. And you will break your silence with a resounding 'yes'.

TRUST THE DKA

A week before opening the bakery, I told the crew I wanted to make *kouign amann*. Everyone's response was the same: 'You want to make *what*?'

The Celtic name looked strange on paper and was even harder to sound out correctly (it's pronounced KWEEN ah-MAHN). Needless to say, from a marketing perspective the team thought it would be a disaster to highlight a little-known, unpronounceable pastry on our menu.

Best described as a 'caramelised croissant', the kouign amann features a dazzling sugary crust and tender croissant-like layers within. Butter, dough and sugar must be perfectly laminated, or layered together—with no intermittent time to chill and rest—to achieve its distinctive crispy, flaky and moist texture.

Within minutes of folding the dough with the butter, the laminated combination adds further challenges as it starts to melt; sprinkling in handfuls of sugar draws out the moisture from the dough. This process leaves many cooks with a soggy mess of indistinguishable layers. It is hard to train someone to pay attention to the minuscule changes of the dough as it endures fold after fold. Containing just a few ingredients—flour, yeast, butter, sugar and water—the kouign amann offers the same challenge as that of an omelet: easy to make, but difficult to make *well*.

Over time, I modified my recipe to decrease the butter and sugar, which resulted in a lighter texture. Removing fat or sugar from any recipe results in a pastry that is more perishable, and this tweak decreased the shelf life of the kouign amann to just twelve hours. Yet another obstacle from the businessman's perspective.

What's more, my recipe required that we prepare a fresh batch every morning. Without any frozen inventory as a safety net, any mistake could ruin the batch and leave the bakery with none to sell for the day.

So which should I have listened to—my head or my gut? It was one of those defining crossroads, and I knew I would regret not giving a product I believed in a chance to win the support of the world. It is easy to ride a trend; it's much harder to move in the opposite direction. That's what we did when we put the DKA on our menu. Every once in a while, you must take a leap of faith.

A day before we welcomed our first customer, I arranged a taste test for the staff in the empty bakery. The next day, when we pulled down the paper from the windows and opened our doors, I could still hear murmurs from behind the register. They were reminiscing about their first taste of 'that caramelised croissant thing'. It became the one pastry that people said was 'life changing'.

Every single kouign amann sold out by noon. Curiosity drove many guests to their first bite, but it was taste that ultimately kept them coming back. Eventually, it became known as the DKA for Dominique's Kouign Amann, a name coined by our regulars for my lightly modified version. The DKA has sold out every day since, and we have quintupled production.

A few days ago a mother and son came to the store. When I asked what their favourite item was, the mother quickly replied, 'The DKA!' And that's when her three-year-old son looked up at me and said, 'Dominique's Kouign Amann,' clearly and with perfect pronunciation.

'IT IS EASY TO RIDE A TREND;
IT'S MUCH HARDER TO MOVE IN THE
OPPOSITE DIRECTION. THAT'S WHAT WE DID
WHEN WE PUT THE DKA ON OUR MENU.'

BREAKING THE SOUFFLÉ LAWS

When executed perfectly, the chocolate soufflé is easy to fall in love with. The spoon cracks the thinly settled top and descends down into the cloud-like chocolate layer, its tip dipping into the molten chocolate beneath.

But what a diva it is! A slammed oven door, a gust in the air and even a whisper could cause its collapse. No other item in a cook's repertoire inspires as much dread. And perhaps that is why it is the only dessert that asserts itself before the rest of your meal has even begun. Order what you will for the main course, but decide up front whether you want to be graced with the presence of the soufflé. Remember the time when every waiter started off the meal cautioning you, 'If you would like to order the soufflé, you would need to place the order *now*.'

I never put a soufflé on my menu when I worked at a restaurant. But that didn't stop regular requests for them, which I always accommodated, if grudgingly. I left my restaurant days behind relishing the fact that I wouldn't have to do another rush order for a chocolate soufflé in the middle of the night for a VIP.

I was recounting my soufflé vexations when I was interrupted. 'What was it about the soufflé that you hated so much?' someone asked. I didn't hate the soufflé, I explained. But I felt restrained by its rigidity. There's only so much you can do to alter a soufflé. It was always the same white ramekin and regular cadre of ingredients: chocolate, raspberries and

so forth. I found it old-fashioned and stuffy. It simply wasn't an innovative dessert. 'Well, I'm sure you could *make* it innovative,' came the response. And the challenge was accepted.

The very next day I set out to create a 'reimagined' soufflé. One that would never collapse and still had the basic characteristics: an aerated crust with an airy and semi-liquid core. I decided to free the soufflé from the confines of its ramekin and make it portable by encasing it in an orange-blossom brioche. It would be one for the rule breakers, the revolutionaries.

This task kept me up nights. Breaking rules, as it turns out, takes a whole lot of work. I studied the technicalities of stabilising egg whites and controlling temperatures, tweaking each step in the execution process. The final product is not something that you can whip together in an instant.'It is laborious and time-consuming. And I'm sure many cooks would prefer the straightforwardness of a classic soufflé recipe rather than the sidesteps in my new version.

But show me a magician who didn't carefully plan each sleight of hand or meticulously calculate the perfectly placed smoke and mirrors so that the trick looks as effortless as when someone rips apart the brioche shell to find a chocolate core. Innovation may seem like magic, but the real triumph is the work behind the scenes.

THE REAL CRONUT™ LESSON

People have a lot to say about the Cronut™ pastry. But they always start off with the same question: 'How did you do it?' And this is quickly followed by: 'How can I do it, too?'

For months, I explained to journalist after journalist that there was no magic formula or marketing strategy behind this croissant-doughnut hybrid. It was simply another creation. I was making a snack for the team who said they wanted to eat doughnuts. Having no recipe for a doughnut, I decided to make my own. Glazed on the top, the pastry was filled with cream and sugared like a doughnut, but it had a laminated dough that was similar to—but not the same as—croissant dough. Crispy on the outside, with tender layers within, it was a playful treat. Two months and ten recipes later, the Cronut pastry was born. Nobody could've imagined what would happen next.

Picasso sketched and painted his whole life, yet only a fraction of his actual body of work became recognisable. Mozart composed since he was a child, but many of us can hum only a few notes from his symphonies. What's more, they both started off not knowing how to

paint or play music at all. And it took every bad sketch and amateur composition to mould them into someone the world applauded. Creativity is about living through *every* creation, even the lacklustre ones. The best creations have makers who are fully immersed in living a creative life. They are all a step forward. I had always believed in that, but inventing the Cronut pastry taught me how to not fall two steps back.

One May morning in 2013, just three days after we launched the Cronut pastry, more than a hundred people were waiting outside the door. The line started three hours before our 8:00 a.m. opening time, and we were just four people inside: two baristas in front and two cooks in the kitchen. 'We're going to do great,' I assured one of the girls working behind the register, trying to swallow the panic bubbling inside me. She had started to tremble at the thought of the crowd bursting through the doors of our small shop in the next few minutes.

Within the cocoon of the bakery walls, we had only heard murmurs of how our humble dessert had 'gone viral' and 'was trending'. Each story was wilder than the next, from a person

who sold a secondhand Cronut pastry for $100 on the black market, to customers offering bribes to our employees, to the sad moments when we caught people going through our trash for whatever rejected portions of the pastry we had tossed out earlier that morning. We were too caught up in trying to do what we could to either gasp in disbelief or rejoice in the success. All we could focus on was getting through the tornado of daily events.

Then came everybody's two cents. Economists spoke of supply meeting demand and urged me to raise my prices. Entrepreneurs gave me lessons on scaling. And there were many who loved dangling the carrot of selling out. There was only one piece of advice I took, and it was simple: 'Imagine what you would have done if the Cronut pastry never existed. Go ahead and do that.'

No matter how steep the climb ahead, the trip is always made easier when you know where you're going. And I had seen my destination in one word: creativity. We moved on. We did the one thing nobody thought we would do—we tried to ignore the Cronut pastry.

We handled matters as we did any other day. Prices were not raised. Large corporations didn't consume us. And growth, although a natural progression in any business, was dealt with mindfully and without rush. Together as a team, we no longer feared the line. We embraced those who waited patiently, with hot chocolate and hand warmers during the winter months and fresh-baked madeleines in the summer. They were serenaded by carollers during the Christmas season and gifted long-stemmed roses on Valentine's Day. We capped our production— not in an effort to make things 'exclusive' but rather as a way to preserve the quality of the product. At one point we had not only moved on, but moved *beyond*. We saw that the Cronut pastry had become a symbol of creativity that drew crowds from around the world, which in turn inspired me to keep working toward my destination and move on to the next creation.

Few things are defined by the moment they were born, but rather the story they lived through. The real secrets lie not in the recipe of the Cronut pastry, but in the infinity that lies ahead of it.

'PEOPLE HAVE A LOT TO SAY ABOUT THE CRONUT™ PASTRY. BUT THEY ALWAYS START OFF WITH THE SAME QUESTION: "HOW DID YOU DO IT?"'

ETERNALLY VANILLA

People ask me all the time what my favourite ice cream flavour is. And when I enthusiastically reply 'Vanilla!' there's always disappointment in their eyes. They seem surprised that I'm not drawn by the vibrant hues of berry-speckled sorbets, nor by the decadent gleam of chocolate or the allure of sea salt on caramel. There is no more competitive battleground for flavours than in an ice cream case.

'You like vanilla?'

They repeat the question, as if giving me a chance to change my mind. Sometimes I suffer a momentary doubt. Should I have said hazelnut or coffee? But then I remind myself: I like vanilla, and I'm not ashamed of it.

We live in a world where twists and turns are applauded. I've had my share of bacon-, avocado- and cheese-flavoured ice creams—most of which I could do without. And a whole year once passed when I didn't eat a scoop of vanilla ice cream. When I finally did, my taste buds, wiped clean of their memory of vanilla, experienced something new. I felt like I was drinking fresh water after a lifetime of wine. Every note rang out clearly.

What has ruined vanilla's reputation isn't that it is used so *widely*, but that it has been used so *poorly*. Oversweetened, extract-flavoured, grainy versions of vanilla ice cream are everywhere. And without a minimum standard, its identity has come to stand for 'plain'. What a sad fate for an exotic black fruit harvested from an orchid.

A truly well-executed vanilla ice cream is a perfect harmony of flavours: the base delicately cooked, the quality of the cream and eggs pristine, and the vanilla pods the very best you can buy. Those floral beans lie over every bite like the softest lace on satin. It isn't Plain Jane. It is Coco Chanel in a room of over-accessorised women, the beauty of Cinderella against her gaudy stepsisters.

Real innovation is not about chasing the fashionable, but having an inherent beauty. It is not about a sampling of cleverness, but honest consideration for what works well. That's vanilla ice cream. If you haven't had it for a while, take a bite of a truly delicious scoop. It's the one flavour that proves itself to be not just a passing fancy, but an eternal romance.

4

··

WHAT'S IN A NAME?

Close to a thousand customers walk through the doors of the bakery daily. I smile or nod as they walk past; our introductions are often brief. The call of the kitchen allows for less time than I would've liked to meet everyone. But there's one encounter I will always remember.

One summer afternoon, a couple approached me. They pointed toward a small photo on the wall of a basket of madeleines. They smiled as they told their story: in a few weeks they would welcome their newborn daughter and they would name her Madeleine. These little cake bites had been the mother's favourite during her pregnancy, and they were hoping for a copy of the photo to hang in the nursery. 'If you could write a note, Chef,' they added with appreciation.

That night I thought about what to write to baby Madeleine. This little girl named after a pastry that was once named after another girl by the name of Madeleine Paulmier, a cook in the eighteenth century. How different yet distinctively 'madeleine' they each are.

The old adage says, 'A picture is worth a thousand words.' To which I always respond: It depends on the word. Names are no ordinary words. Names precede us, oftentimes long before we are even born, and survive after we have died. Few people know that my real name is actually Dominique Ansel Jr. I was named after my father, but I never thought of it as something to live up to. We could not be more different. For me, the name was a blessing. It reminded me of the love he had for me.

Over the years, there are many 'nameless' creations I have placed on my menu. I merely described what they were—a fruit tart, a piece of cake. But in this chapter, I will highlight creations that were brought to life with a name. Sometimes a name leads to a specific set of expectations, like the Perfect Little Egg Sandwich. Other times a name can unlock a deeper history, as it was for the *religieuse*. Names can also be transporting,

especially when they draw inspiration from places, like my interpretation of the Paris-Brest. And I explain how a quick abbreviation, which resulted in the Mini Me, can give a pastry new purpose in the kitchen.

When I handed over the photo of the madeleines to the couple the next day, I had written a message that only Madeleine and her parents would know for the years to come. The most important words were the first two. 'To Madeleine,' it began. And that was worth more than a thousand words already.

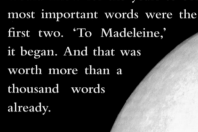

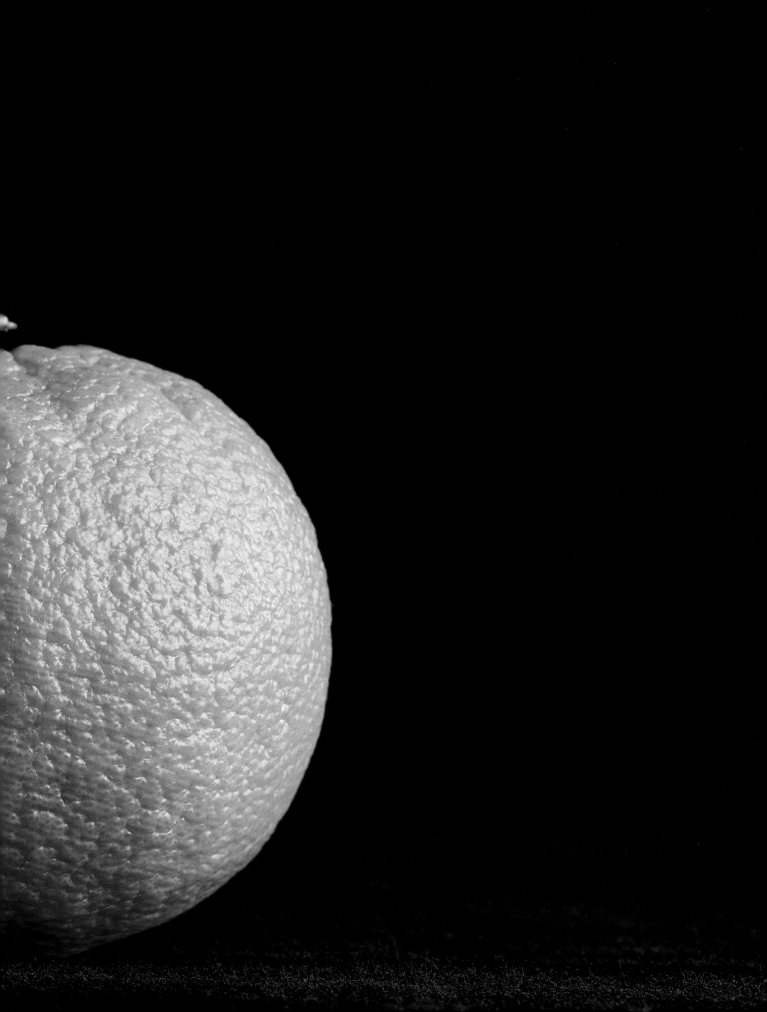

PERFECTING A LITTLE EGG SANDWICH

'The Perfect Little Egg Sandwich,' I scribbled on a Post-it note.

It was the first thing that our first customer ordered when the bakery opened. I welcomed him into the brand-new shop and carefully assembled it myself: a fluffy, two-inch-thick slice of warm scrambled eggs, seasoned with caramelised spring onions, chives, and a liberal sprinkling of sea salt and ground black pepper; a paper-thin slice of Gruyère cheese, slightly melted under the grill; all between a freshly toasted, buttery brioche bun. *Simple*, I thought.

But the word 'perfect' changes everything. It is a monumental title for a humble creation to live up to.

'Is it *really* perfect?' the skeptics asked. 'What makes it perfect?' the theorists wondered.

After a while, even I started to question the whole idea of perfection. I threw myself back into the kitchen in an attempt to make the sandwich *more* perfect. What if I added bacon or pancetta? Maybe some sort of spread over the bread? As winter rolled around, I even created a version of the sandwich with fresh black truffles.

When our first customer—now a regular— returned for his daily breakfast sandwich, I was eager to show him the new option. 'Would you like to try the one with the black truffle?' our staff suggested.

'No,' he said, 'just the perfect is fine.' He said it in a nonchalant way. But his answer was a wake-up call.

Perhaps the platonic ideal of the perfect little egg sandwich doesn't exist. The idea of a flawless state is a static one. And it suggests that nothing can be improved upon. In that sense it feels a bit limited; it's the end of the road. Being perfect may not be the real goal in the end, but *becoming* perfect is filled with the promise of always progressing. When I thought about perfection as a quest, I let go of the stress of expectations. Instead, I was filled with infinite inspiration. In my mind I placed the word 'perfect' silently in front of every new creation I attempted. When you no longer fear perfection, you set loftier goals and surprisingly accomplish more than you think you might. Creations break, they stall, there's always a better version to be made. But few creations are ever great unless they first aspire to be perfect.

DRESS UP WITH THE RELIGIEUSE

When I teach my staff how to make the *religieuse*, I always tell them the story behind the pastry. This two-tiered cream puff, dipped into dark chocolate glaze and piped with white butter-cream, earned its name because it resembles the black-and-white headdress of a nun.

'Do you see the way it kind of looks like a woman's head and body?' I say.

'Yes,' they respond.

'And it's dressed like a nun.' That is always followed by a chuckle.

I never understood why they laugh. The explanation seemed second nature to me, since this classic pastry can be found in just about every bakery in France. I had grown up loving this double-decker delight, staring at it in the cases of the Dalloyau pastry shops. Filled with different flavours of pastry cream, it always seemed a decadent alternative to the éclair. But in New York, few had heard of this treat. And we never sold as many religieuses as I hoped.

Then I finally got the joke. How sad was it that the religieuse had been dressed up as a nun for all these years! It seemed prim and unapproachable when desserts were supposed to be just the opposite—sensual and seductive.

It was New York Fashion Week at the time,

and so I decided to dress up the religieuse after years of its fashion conservatism. Ruffles and pale white flowers on one, a scarlet glaze and piped lace décor on another, and a black-and-white dandy approach on a third.

Names can be constricting. And sometimes we have to put those names aside and appreciate what lies beneath. Once I saw the religieuse as a body form to dress, anything was possible. We did Valentine's Day angel religieuses and Santa religieuses. They were topped in berets for Bastille Day and witch hats for Halloween. Customers forgot about the name 'religieuse' and identified with what they saw in front of them. Within weeks of this breakthrough, we catered our first wedding with religieuses dressed as brides and grooms. Every one of its incarnations became a top seller at the bakery. It is a tradition we continue to this day.

We're not always given the honor of naming a creation. Classics come with their own title, personality and history. Understanding a creation means embracing its past, but also letting it become a foundation for a more relevant present. It is something that doesn't need to be shed, but once in a while, things can be redressed.

A NEW YORK PASTRY

'Where are you from?' asked the cabdriver as we crossed the Queensborough Bridge toward Manhattan. It was a straightforward question to which I always answered: France. But that day, the answer changed. 'I'm from New York,' I said.

We always remember the first time we meet the people who will later change our lives. We look back at the formal introductions, the shyness and the serendipity that brought us all together. I remember meeting New York for the first time, and it was the closest I've ever experienced to love at first sight.

Never had I seen a city that was so alive. The constant flow of people and cars pulsates through the streets with each pounding heartbeat. The skyscrapers stretch upward with the dreams of the city. And every corner can be reborn in the blink of an eye to showcase a new shop, new restaurant and new idea. New York is the mother of reinvention, the consummate muse; she's everyone's paramour, and as one of my biggest inspirations, I wanted to capture her in a dessert.

But what does New York 'taste' like? I started to list the flavours that reminded me of this city. The burnt caramel scent of street-side vendors roasting nuts in the winter as you exit the subway stations. That aroma of hazelnut coffee drifting from every corner deli. The brininess of hot dogs mixing with the tinge of sauerkraut. A garlicky stir-fry hitting the sizzling woks in Chinatown. The sweet, yeasty air of bagel shops. The bubbling mozzarella fresh out of pizza ovens. Every thought took me down a different street. Trying to pinpoint a taste for one of the most eclectic cities in the world was an impossible task.

It's as if you were trying to explain all the reasons you love someone. You would produce an endless list that never quite expresses the vastness of your feelings.

So I went back to that very first time I met New York. The plane ride here had been long and sleepless as I sat awake in anxious thought. It was the calm before the storm of being ushered through immigration and baggage claim and finally pushed outdoors, where I remember squinting at the blue skies and breathing in the cold air. Before hopping into a cab, I bought a Snickers bar. I took bite after bite of the caramel, peanut and chocolate treat as we drove toward the skyline made so clearly recognisable by the Empire State Building.

The dessert I dedicated to New York is called the Paris–New York. Inspired by that simple chocolate bar that became my first 'meal' in the city, I built it by piping concentric rings of soft caramel, milk chocolate and peanut butter ganache. It is a take on the Paris-Brest, traditionally a ring of choux pastry dough filled with hazelnut cream. The Paris-Brest was named after a bicycle race that runs between the two cities: Paris to Brest, then back to Paris. What better way to capture my journey than creating a Paris–New York?

I could never distill the ever-changing New York down to a few flavours. And so many objects of inspiration are not captured completely in the creations that are tributes to them. My trick is to always zoom in: that little bit of glitter is all you need. Even if you manage to express just the tip of what something means to you, it's worth a shot.

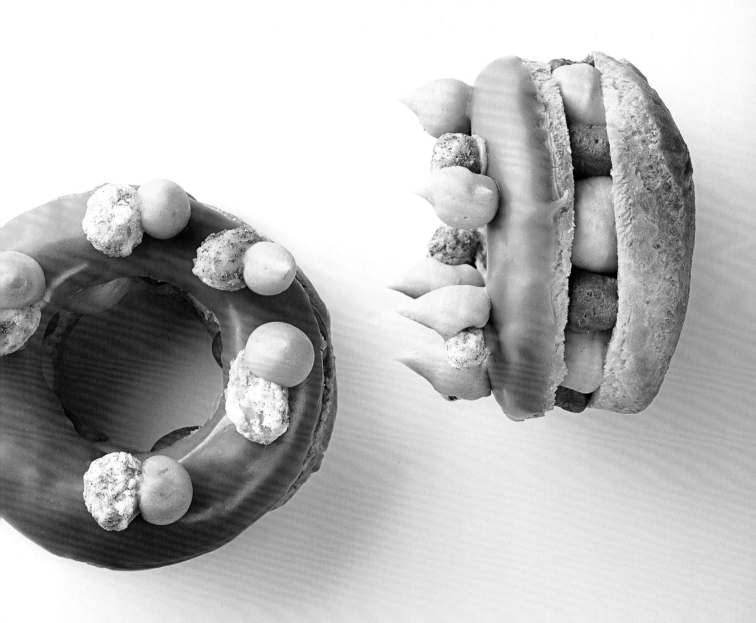

ME, MINI ME AND MERINGUES

I wasn't planning on talking about work when I met up with my friend Aun, who was visiting from Singapore, for lunch. But somewhere between our appetiser and main course, I told him that I was interested in making a line of miniature meringues piped in tiny teardrops as a takeaway gift item. I wanted them to be cute and playful. The only problem was 'miniature meringues'—the name—was neither.

'Meringuettes', 'meringue kisses', 'petites meringues'—I listed the rejects for him to hear.

'What about Mini Me?' he suggested, alluding to the famous character in *Austin Powers*. The problem of naming these meringues was instantly solved. We both knew this would be the name. Aun had managed to think of something in thirty seconds that I had struggled for three months to figure out. If only every part of the creative process could be as easy as this.

What do you imagine when you picture an innovator? A mad scientist secretly mixing potions in his lab? An author crinkling up page after page of written text in a struggle to find the right words? A programmer hunched over her screen with her fingers pounding out code?

Most of the time, we tend to think of creativity as a solo enterprise. We are taught that it requires silence, privacy and time to incubate. An idea is fragile—the slightest snicker might dissuade its owner from transforming thought into action. Yet sometimes, when we open up to the rest of the world, we are able to break our own boundaries. Inspiration doesn't happen in a locked room. In my case, it happened in a bustling restaurant with a round of drinks on the table.

Aun was back in Singapore long before the Mini Me's launched. He never got to taste them or see them sitting on the bakery's shelves. But he had proven to me that creativity can be a social affair. The key is in finding the right confidant whose opinions and taste you respect and realising that opening yourself up to others can bring a new perspective to a challenge. Two can often be better than one.

What was so brilliant about Aun's suggestion wasn't just the humour behind it, but the fact that the name also suggested a function. I realised that the Mini Me's shouldn't be in name only. I made them the *mignons* for other desserts. I would add them to cakes, sprinkle them over ice cream, drop them into hot chocolate. They were no longer a stand-alone confection, but a companion to so many others. It was an item that elevated those around it, the way that sometimes people around you can do the same for you.

'I REALISED THAT THE MINI ME'S SHOULDN'T BE IN
NAME ONLY. I MADE THEM THE *MIGNONS* FOR OTHER DESSERTS.
THEY WERE NO LONGER A STAND-ALONE CONFECTION,
BUT A COMPANION TO SO MANY OTHERS.'

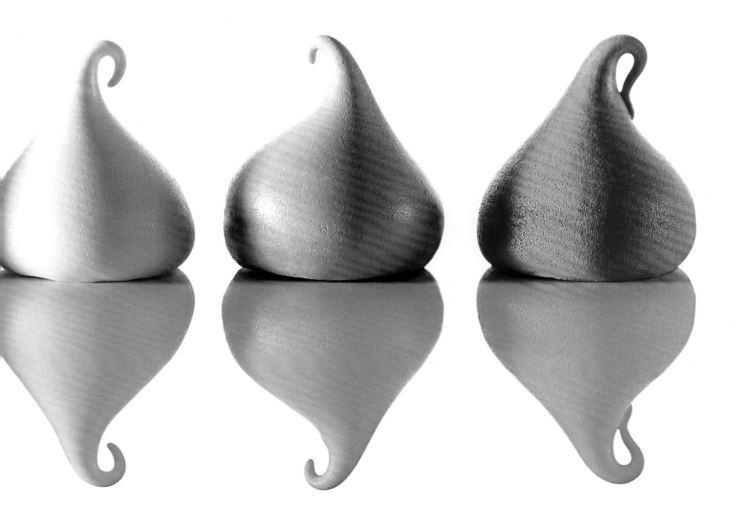

5

CREATE AND RE-CREATE

It's a make-or-break moment for any pastry chef: the few seconds after you finish your showpiece and begin the stunt of moving it to the display table. A showpiece, made out of chocolate or sugar, does just what its name suggests—it shows off. Paper-thin sugar ribbons, delicate chocolate spires, it's a demonstration of skill and prowess. The goal is to defy gravity. The slightest bump can unleash an avalanche of falling pieces and result in the deepest of heartbreak.

Three cooks helped me carry my show-piece. With carefully choreographed steps, we all held our breath until the moment when the final fingertip pulled away from beneath the structure. I had assembled a large chocolate wave that wove around and back onto itself. It doubled as a display piece and a stand for my desserts. The structure required close to 220 pounds (100 kilograms) of chocolate to create. It took three weeks to perfect.

A few hours after its debut, however, I bashed my chocolate sculpture with a hammer like a wrecking ball through a wall. Those around me gasped as I knocked the pieces until splintered bits of chocolate covered the table.

'How can you stand to break down something you worked so hard to build?' one observer asked. To which I explained that I wasn't breaking down, I was getting ready to build back up. This was the process of re-creation.

Chocolate, which can be melted and re-sculpted endlessly, is one of my favourite ingredients. I love to watch the sculpted shapes melt into a smooth and glossy pool, once again becoming a tabula rasa. Certain mediums constantly welcome reinvention. After each appearance, they can be reincarnated. They form a new and different wonder.

This chapter is about breaking down the classics and building them back up. Certain pastries have long-forgotten histories, and when you rediscover their secrets, you find inspiration for new points of view, as was the case with my Cotton-Soft Cheesecake. I'll tell you about how something as storied as a croissant can be transformed in what seems like a magic trick. Sometimes, I'm inspired by things I don't particularly like, and I'll explain how when I describe my apple tarte tatin. Finally, I'll share my story about how a bite-size *chouquette*, a small, unfilled cream puff, earned a spot in people's hearts thanks to another one-bite treat.

We're often told that we shouldn't try to fix what's not broken. I'm not trying to 'fix' anything. Instead, I see each and every creation and re-creation as unique. There is no end to the road. Think instead of the endless number of paths, and open your mind to what lies beyond the horizon.

A few months after I smashed it, I recast my chocolate wave showpiece as an Easter egg the size of my torso. When May rolled around, I broke it down and shaped it into chocolate flower petals for a cake display. Some of these re-creations were big, others were small. Some were sturdy, others were more delicate. The beauty, however, is in how they were all connected.

THE CHEESECAKE'S
FORGOTTEN HERITAGE

Who invented the first cheesecake? Would you have guessed the Greeks?

I was shocked to learn this bit of trivia. For me, it seemed like an American classic. But it was the Romans who adopted the original cheesecake from the Greeks and spread it throughout Europe as their empire expanded. And when Europeans later landed on the shores of a newly discovered America, they brought the recipe with them. This plain-looking dessert, consisting of a cheese-based filling in a pastry shell, had been served on the table of Olympic athletes, emperors and immigrants.

Today, you can find cheesecake all over the world. In every location there's a different twist. Chicago-style cheesecakes tend to use sour cream. The Germans prefer quark instead of cream cheese. And in Japan, the filling is made with a touch of cornstarch so that it whips to a light consistency. But perhaps the best known of all is the New York–style cheesecake: a dense cream cheese filling, slightly browned on top, and a graham cracker crust on the bottom. It is the bold 'original' standard for so many.

'If you live in New York, you have to do a cheesecake,' I was told. At one point, virtually every restaurant had a cheesecake on its menu. But my quest would be to approach it from a different angle.

It was the cheesecake's forgotten heritage that became my inspiration. Our shop in SoHo is within walking distance of some of the most eclectic neighbourhoods in the city. Seeing freshly made ricotta draining in cheesecloth a few blocks east in Little Italy set off the spark that would lead me to develop a light ricotta mousse filling for my cheesecake. Tasting a warm almond sponge cake on a cold winter day in Chinatown, just to the south, gave me the vision of a moist almond cake base in lieu of the expected graham cracker one. The final touch, a slightly torched sugar crust over the cheesecake, came from a dessert every Frenchman grew up with—the crème brûlée.

My Cotton-Soft Cheesecake never goes off the bakery's menu. It is not the classic New York–style cheesecake. But then again, New York–style cheesecake is nothing like the original Greek-style cheesecake, which used fresh cheese that was pounded with a stone into a paste. A pair of denim jeans has changed its cut and wash throughout the decades but maintained its integrity. Automobiles have become slicker and more modern than their original models. Even constitutions in countries undergo amendments and modifications. Classics don't resist change; they are built on it.

SWITCHING OUT HAM FOR JAMÓN

The street performer held a coin up to my eye level and warned me not to blink. Without breaking my stare, I watched as he twisted his fingers and transformed one coin into two. My jaw dropped. I was just a boy. It was the first time I witnessed magic.

These days I see magic in every creation—whether it's a piece of music, a daring work of architecture, or a delicious new pastry. And there are always three parts to this magic trick. The first is a sense of wonder.

'I wonder if we could do that?' Seamus asked me. As the chef of the award-winning Spanish restaurant Tertulia, located a few blocks away in the West Village, he had dropped by to visit the bakery. He wanted to know if we could re-create the classic ham and cheese croissant into something with a Spanish flair, using *jamón ibérico*, a cured ham from the black-footed Iberian pig, and aged Mahón cheese.

I never thought of modifying our ham and cheese croissant before that moment. When you're inside a kitchen working with the same pantry of ingredients, sometimes it takes an outsider to inspire a sense of wonder.

The second part of the magic trick is delivering the result. To wonder freely without putting an idea into action is but to daydream. All miracles take work. It took me a whole month to figure out how I could make the most of these new ingredients. It might have been easier to simply fold the new ham and cheese into the croissant dough. That is the way it is always done. But working with such special (and pricey) products pushed me to do more. In order to maximise the flavour of the *jamón ibérico*, which is sliced much thinner than traditional Parisian *jambon*, I incorporated the lard, which carries that signature deep nuttiness, into the butter package for the dough. And I added in trimmings and flakes of the *jamón* so you could see it speckled throughout the crumb of the *viennoiserie*. At every step, I tested and tweaked to preserve the croissant's light, flaky texture. We sent a test batch over to Seamus's kitchen and awaited a response. An email hit our inbox a few hours later filled with exclamation marks.

And that's when we prepare for the last part of the magic trick: delight. The first time a stranger, completely unaware of the weight of the work it took, simply takes a bite. I wait for it, as I'm sure the magician did when he first dazzled me on the street corner. It's a moment of joy that plays in front of me in slow motion when a customer's lips press together in a deep purr of 'Mmm . . .'

Often right after my guests taste something, they want to know the recipe and story behind it. 'Show me how to do this magic trick,' they say. I'm happy to share, but always hesitate for a moment. The reveal is an illuminating yet disheartening process: once you explain the steps and the labour, the fantasy dissipates. But I always find comfort in the fact that perhaps this person might use this knowledge to fascinate someone else. We can all pay it forward with magic.

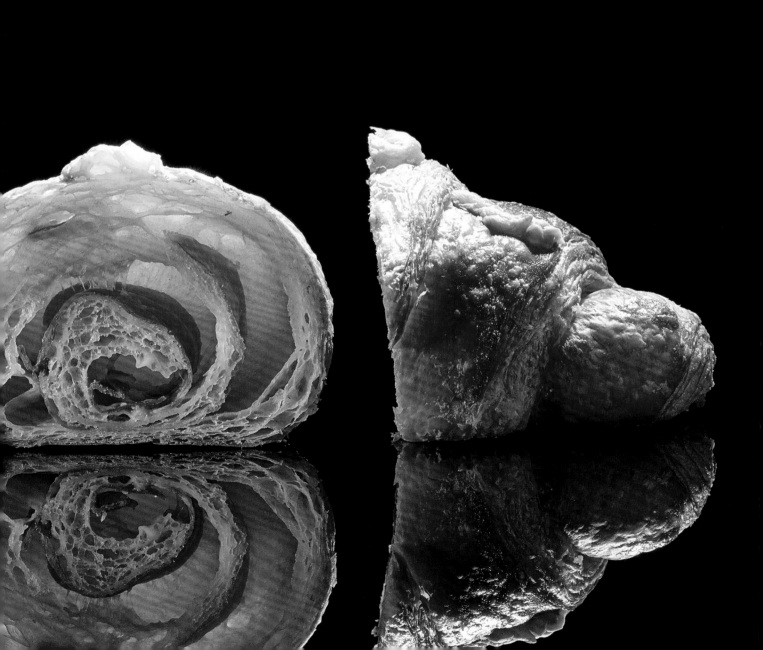

THE APPLE TART OF MY EYE

When I was a young boy, my parents brought me to the street carnivals in France, where I spent entire afternoons trying my hand at every coin toss and shooting game before jumping on the Ferris wheel to catch the sunset. But while my siblings scarfed down their *pommes d'amour*, a candied apple treat found at every fair, with delight, I never quite felt the same.

At first, the pomme d'amour was tempting. The scarlet caramel shell glistened as if made from blown glass. A whole apple promised a decadent—and generous—serving. But the illusion was shattered when I took my first bite. The tough skin of the apple wedged between my front teeth. Sour juice ran down my chin as I struggled to keep pieces of tacky caramel from falling on—and staining—my clothes. I was embarrassed to come clean to my family about how much I didn't like this well-loved treat. I didn't want to seem unappreciative. It always feels as if you're living in a different world when you don't agree with popular opinion.

Years later, when I was in my teens, I bit my tongue as well when a waiter suggested I order the apple tarte tatin. At the time, the tarte tatin was the most in-demand restaurant dessert. Made with thick apple segments gently sautéed in a deep caramel and topped with a buttery puff pastry crust, the whole thing was then flipped upside down and displayed with a big voilà at the table.

Eyes widened as my dining companions prepared to dig into the sumptuous dish. But for my taste? It was a little too sweet. The apples, saturated with an intense amount of caramel, tasted like candy rather than fruit, and their texture was mushy from a prolonged cooking time. Yet it was such an iconic dish I felt almost guilty for not liking it.

Opinions come in waves and with the support of the masses, but it's okay to think differently. Try not to let your own thoughts be drowned out by the voices of the crowd. Understanding your own head, your own heart—that is the first step to creating something you will stand behind. I eventually confessed my true feelings about these two desserts. But I took it one step further. I pinpointed the problems and examined the flaws with a constructive eye.

One day in my kitchen, I decided that I would make an apple tarte tatin my way. Rather than cutting the apples into segments as was traditionally done, I peeled each apple delicately and kept it whole. A memory of the pomme d'amour flashed in my mind. I remembered how the possibility of eating a whole apple had been so alluring. And when I baked the entire apple in its own mould, I discovered that this eliminated the problem of oversweetening the fruit with caramel. Even when baked through, the inner core would retain the juiciness and the firmness of a fresh apple. When I stepped back and took a victorious bite of my tweaked version, I realised that I had used two desserts that I disliked as inspiration to create one that I love. If you don't like something, don't avoid it—improve it.

ONE BITE OF CHOUQUETTE

There's one item you can find in *every* bakery in France, but not a single French bakery in New York. *Chouquettes* are tiny balls of *pâte à choux*, the egg-based dough that makes up the base of éclairs and cream puffs. They are left unfilled and speckled with pearl sugar granules that look like white polka dots from a distance.

Bakers traditionally used leftover batter from other choux dough–based pastries to make basketfuls of chouquettes. And while buying breads and viennoiseries in France, I'd always add on an order of chouquettes as a snack. Sold by weight in some places and in batches of ten or twenty in others, the shopkeeper shovelled these treats into a wax paper bag with a large scoop, and I would happily pop them in my mouth on the way home.

It was not a delicate product. Without fancy shapes, fillings or adornments, chouquettes seldom sat in the prime location on the display counter. But something about the way the pearl sugar crunched slightly with each bite won my heart. And the light, popover-like texture—toasted on the outside and eggy and soft within—made them so easy to eat. Bite by bite, I'd empty a whole bag without realising it.

The chouquettes were a hard sell to New Yorkers who hadn't grown up with them. Customers always seemed disappointed to find out that it was 'nothing special'. It didn't promise to open new doors to flavours and textures. It didn't dazzle. *No wonder it never became popular in the United States,* I thought. But the question I couldn't stop asking myself was: *How did it become so popular in France?*

Toward the end of each day in the bakery, I had a habit of looking at which pastries were

the last to sell out. Predictably, the chouquette was one of them. One day, fifteen minutes before the doors closed, a couple walked in and perused our final offerings—and both picked an order of ten chouquettes. They politely asked our cashier to help service them more quickly as they were trying to catch a movie that was starting soon in the theatre up the block.

A lightbulb went on in my head. The chouquette wasn't similar to any bakery item I had seen in New York, but it was very similar to one item offered in every movie theatre throughout the city: popcorn. The ritual of eating both was similar. You carry it in a bag. You munch on a few while doing something else. It was something that was casual, to be enjoyed without consuming your full attention, like a pleasant soundtrack playing in the background.

From that day on, I combined these two treats, using the crunch of caramelised popcorn kernels to add further texture to the chouquettes. And bite by bite, the customers hopped on the bandwagon.

Sometimes, the key to creation is the process of hunting for natural compatibilities. Like matchmaking, we search for soul mates. And though popcorn and chouquettes come from different fields, cultures and even times, our senses confirmed that they belonged together.

When the chouquettes were removed from the menu to make room for new offerings, they became one of the things our regulars often ask for to this day. 'I never really knew about it before I tried it here,' a customer told me. 'But something made me feel like I had been eating it all my life.'

6

EVERYTHING
BUT
THE FLAVOUR

One winter, I had one of those flus that wouldn't go away. And while a small sinus problem is unpleasant for anyone, for a chef it can be debilitating. I could no longer detect the depth and complexity of sweet, salty, sour and bitter on my tongue. Take a bite of an apple and an onion the next time you have a stuffy nose. You'll find them indistinguishable.

Like the plot to a tragedy, I was a chef who could not taste. But then things started to change. The human mind and body evolve and compensate. If you lose sight in one eye, your vision in the other naturally adjusts. Knock out one sense, and the others intensify. And just as closing your eyes helps you hear your surroundings better, I began to see this disadvantage as an opportunity to focus on more subtle aspects of food.

When you read a restaurant review, so much of what is described is the flavour of each dish. Does grapefruit work well with chocolate? Would it be a better match with rosemary? How was the seasoning? These are the types of decisions on ingredients and seasoning chefs consider daily. But when you can't taste, you start to notice all the other traits.

This chapter is about things you may have once overlooked. By leaving customers in the dark about the specific ingredients in my Sunflower Tart, I let them experience an entirely new spectrum of flavours. I recount the story of the Frozen S'more, my take on a nostalgic campfire treat, and how a wooden branch helped me redefine boundaries. Substitutes are common in recipes, but in the story of the much-loved Mont Blanc and its signature tower of chestnut cream, the ingredient that is the substitute becomes the star. I explain how certain flavours taste 'warm' with my version of a baked Alaska, and reveal my quest to find a taste for the colour purple in the Purple Tart. And last, I talk about the *arlette*, a magnificent cookie whose fragility is its strength.

Sometimes we can suffer from a case of nearsightedness. In concerts, we zoom in on the lead vocalist and forget the band that supports him or her. We notice the vibrant red roses in a bouquet before we appreciate the baby's breath that buffers them. We're often blinded by the obvious. In this chapter, I find inspiration in what's often ignored.

I couldn't cook as I recovered from the flu. All I could do was think. Before bed, I jotted down some ideas for new desserts. When my senses finally recovered, I returned to the kitchen and had my first official taste test. They became some of my favourite creations to date.

THE SUNFLOWER TART ILLUSION

A few years ago, I drank an amazing cup of hot chocolate. It had a distinctive nuttiness, as if the cocoa beans had been roasted fresh that morning. After I made a few attempts to discern the type of chocolate they used, the chef finally told me that the 'secret' was caramel. There was absolutely nothing extraordinary about adding caramel to hot chocolate, but the fact that they hadn't specified it was a *caramel* hot chocolate made the touch unexpected. Without the description, the familiar flavour was hard to pinpoint. Until someone pointed it out. I took another sip of the hot chocolate, and there it was—I could taste the caramel notes distinctly.

How the wheels in the mind begin to turn before any food hits the tongue, I thought. The briefest encounter can leave deep-rooted memories—particularly when it comes to taste. Mention an ingredient and we can't help but process, project and expand upon it. As a courtesy, I had always thought it good practice to list the key ingredients of my desserts for customers. But on the day I created the Sunflower Tart, I broke this habit.

The Sunflower Tart, contrary to its name, did not contain any sunflower seeds—or in fact anything related to a sunflower. Rather, it was a moniker based purely on aesthetics. Thin, mandoline-sliced pieces of ripe fruit surrounded a gelée centre that was adorned with a sprinkling of poppy seeds. Assembled with an ombré of orange, gold and auburn tones from the fruit, the tart resembled its eponymous flower and was a tantalising sight to behold.

But just what was in it? The ingredients were 'secret' and, surprisingly, very few customers asked. When I asked them to guess what the ingredients were on their own, the answers were fascinating. Without any guidelines, they picked up notes of lavender and violet, melon and butter, and all sorts of exotic blossoms and fruits. In reality, the tart was a combination of passionfruit, apricot and honey. I added a hint of a spice blend that contained lemon peel, saffron and peppercorn, which amplified the ripeness of the fruit.

Passionfruit and apricot are not unusual flavours in the pastry world; they're a natural pair with their balance of sweet and tart. But with its ingredients unstated and description minimal, the unassuming tart inspired my customers to project layer after layer of extra flavours. The final touch of imagination in any creation can sometimes be left to be filled in by someone else. Keeping things 'secret' is not so much about protection as it is about exploration. The unknown is a wildly imaginative place.

The s'more has always caught my eye. The mesmerising way the amber char spreads across the surface of the marshmallow as it roasts over the fire. How the white core oozes under the pressure of the graham crackers sandwiching it. And how the molten chocolate peeks out from the bottom as the heat begins to melt it.

What really stole my attention, however, was the wooden branch sticking through the marshmallow as it roasted over the fire. It made for a tool for both cooking and eating—a handle with a real functional significance: it made the s'more finger-friendly and fun. A marshmallow on a fork or plate would never carry that same spirit.

One summer, New York experienced record-breaking temperatures in an excruciating heat wave that lasted throughout July. Most of the customers wanted lemonade and couldn't stomach much more. Walking down the street from the store beneath the blistering sun, I began to notice a whole lot of people holding ice cream cones and iceblocks. Ice cream cones and iceblocks conveniently came with their own handle. *So does the s'more,* I thought.

Back in the kitchen, I began to work on an ice cream version of the s'more to stand up to these summertime treats. The first step was to create a marshmallow that wouldn't freeze solid but would remain chewy with the help of honey instead of sugar. Within it, I created a core of soft vanilla ice cream coated with chocolate-covered *feuilletine* to mimic the crunch of graham crackers and provide a hint of chocolate. The whole thing was then skewered with a willow wood branch, which I smoked with apple wood to mimic the smell of a campfire. Each Frozen S'more was then torched to order for customers.

Seeing toasted marshmallows on branches being carried down the SoHo streets in the middle of a summer day was surreal. It intrigued anyone who passed by to ask what the very familiar yet seemingly out-of-place item was. All this from a humble wooden branch.

The world speaks to each of us in a particular language. You see a puddle on the street and simply jump over it, but a photographer might stop and appreciate the beauty of the sky's reflection within it. A pretty girl turns your head while a fashion designer raises an eye to acknowledge the drape of her dress. When we immerse ourselves in a specific field, we learn the cadences of that particular language. I look at a s'more and see not just how it's made, but how it *could* be made. Experience and expertise help us transform from appreciators to creators who see endless possibility.

'I LOOK AT A S'MORE AND
SEE NOT JUST HOW IT'S MADE,
BUT HOW IT *COULD* BE MADE.'

A SWEET POTATO SUBSTITUTE

The word 'substitute' induces an instant headache for any chef.

Here at the bakery, we always try our best to accommodate. We replace flour with gluten-free alternatives; we cut out nuts when we can. The extra step, the added effort—that was never what vexed me about substitutes. What I hated was the stigma around the backup ingredient. Substitutes result from limitations; they are seen as secondary to the original. A substitute suggests it's not 'the way it was intended to be'.

Around the time of writing this book, I became fascinated with the idea of substitutes. I understood their place and necessity in certain recipes. Take the classic French Mont Blanc, a pastry named after a famous mountain and interpreted through a tower of chestnut cream surrounding meringue, orange marmalade and whipped cream. We source our chestnuts directly from Aubenas in France every autumn and winter, but as I was writing the list of ingredients to include in this recipe, I wondered whether the home cook could find them in a supermarket in the States.

Months later, lost in thought at the dinner table on Thanksgiving Day, I took bite after bite of candied sweet potato. And in a moment of clarity, I realised the textural similarities between that and chestnut purée. Both were smooth, creamy and slightly sweet. But only one had the added benefit of being accessible to the home cook.

I woke up the next morning and headed immediately to the kitchen to create a Sweet Potato Mont Blanc. Never had I experienced an ingredient that so naturally adopted its new role. The striking colour of the cream as I moulded it into the shape of a mountain peak looked like the terra-cotta of the Rockies rather than the harsher grey rocks of Mont Blanc. The sweet potato cream blended seamlessly with the orange marmalade and meringue. And there was a buttery quality to the mixture that surpassed the version I made with chestnuts.

What began as a substitute ingredient ended up as the hero for my new autumn dessert. With the more familiar ingredient, customers who were once intimidated by the Mont Blanc now enjoyed the new incarnation. The Sweet Potato Mont Blanc was received like a star, rather than an understudy.

This dessert taught me to be wary of judging ingredients prematurely. It's a lesson that has carried over to all aspects of my life. I try not to put too much stock in reputations. They so easily undercut an ingredient's—or a person's—potential. Many of the most famous singers today started off as backup for a then-more-popular band. Great men were once assistants to someone else. Just because one item or topic isn't playing a key role now doesn't mean it won't excel in the future. Every inspiration is looking for its big break.

BAKING PIE IN ALASKA

'What makes the desert beautiful,' said the Little Prince in Antoine de Saint-Exupéry's novel, 'is that somewhere it hides a well.' It's one of the few lines I can recall from reading the book in school. Something about it made me dream. An oasis, hidden within the sandy dunes of the desert, is the perfect metaphor for hope and possibility.

I thought of this quote when I first tasted the baked Alaska. It came to the table roaring with flames. I watched the meringue slowly darken and flambé under its fiery halo. But while its entrance was grand, the dessert turned out to be rather bland.

'It pretty much just tastes like sponge cake and ice cream," my dining companion said. She dispelled the fantasy as I took my first bite. But I wasn't content to let that be. *The promise of fire and ice holds so much potential,* I thought. I was determined to find a way to carry these flavours beyond the baked Alaska's surface. For weeks, I approached this challenge like a Rubik's cube, shifting blocks to try to match up the pieces.

I began to research how food scientists made hot ice cream. Reading volumes of experiments, I learned how to use food gums and hydrocolloids with unpronounceable names. The bizarre, foreign ingredients in molecular gastronomy had always intrigued but intimidated me.

Finally, I took a step back. I was focusing on the science rather than the taste. I had forgotten that certain ingredients naturally 'taste' like a temperature. Mint feels cooling to the throat even after being steeped in hot water for tea. Chilli flakes add heat to a cold salad. And the beauty of these ingredients is that not one of them was manufactured in a lab.

With four flavours of ice cream and sorbet—green apple Calvados, caramel, smoked cinnamon and vanilla—I constructed the flavours of my baked Alaska. I toasted salted-butter cookies to coat the bottom and sides. When I was done, I shared my creation with my team. 'It tastes like a warm apple pie à la mode,' one person said. Of course, the dessert wasn't served warm, but I understood exactly what she meant.

We're taught in this world that nothing worthwhile comes easily, and so we often assume that the difficult path is the right one. But as I struggled to improve the baked Alaska, I realised that to make something better, you don't always have to rip it apart. Instead, if you identify the right tweaks, you can effect great change with the smallest gesture. You just have to wander in a desert for a while to find an oasis.

I once heard a story about astronauts, which may or may not be true. Up in space, they struggled to write with ballpoint pens, which no longer worked without gravity to pull down the ink. Engineers started to develop specialised space pens that were pressurised chambers and could write on ceilings on earth, too. But the simpler solution, of course, was just to use a pencil.

WHAT PURPLE TASTES LIKE

We live in a colourful world, and our minds are constantly interpreting what these colours mean. You pick through the mangoes stacked on the supermarket shelves to find a rich orange skin that signifies the fruit is ripe for eating. Faint specks of green warn you that the bread is rotten. The deepening amber as caramel cooks reads like a thermometer and lets you know to take the pot off the heat before the caramel turns bitter from burning. When it comes to food, colour has always been an indicator of what's to come. But what does the colour actually *taste* like?

Early autumn is harvest season in upstate New York. And one October, I was lucky to spend an afternoon combing through the bushes to pick fresh blackberries at a farm. Driving back into the city, I snacked on a carton of blackberries and returned to the bakery to find my hands, teeth and tongue stained an inky purple. It gave me the idea for the Purple Tart.

The dessert features a combination of blackberries, dark plums and Concord grapes. The fruits are seldom used in a recipe together, but with my newfound appreciation for colour, they seemed to belong in the same family. I tasted each one carefully. Purple fruits aren't exactly sweet, as is the case with red strawberries or raspberries. They all shared a light edge from the tannins of the skin and a deep, wine-like flavour. Colour coordinating became a new way to discover compatible tastes.

Our eyes trump our taste buds when it comes to colour, and we forget how colour affects our sense of taste as well as our sight.

We've all *tasted* colour—think of the raw, vegetal taste of chlorophyll from green fruits. The Purple Tart reminded me to use all my senses, and to think with my eyes, ears, fingers, nose and taste buds to make connections between ingredients I hadn't before.

Poets describe words as sweet and hearts as full. Perfumers create scents that smell beautiful. What if we could understand what it is like to hear a sunset or see music? Imagine what the future holds if we access it with all our senses.

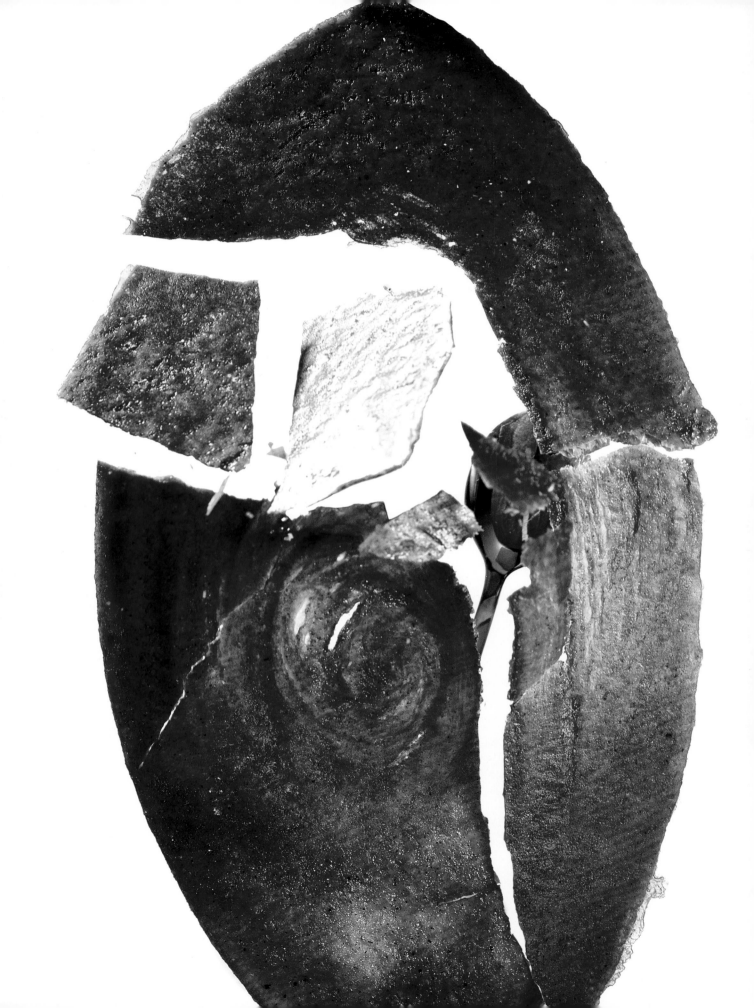

THE BREAKABLE ARLETTE

What type of watch do you wear—digital or mechanical? If it is the latter, ask yourself why. A mechanical watch is a device from an older generation. Many are not waterproof; they are less accurate and come with fewer added functions. The digital watch, with its slicker shape and more convenient use, was meant to be a modern alternative. It is less costly and more durable, and even offers more wearable comfort. But why is it that digital watches haven't completely replaced the classic mechanical watch?

The answer to that question led me to the *arlette*. The lesser-known cousin of a palmier, the arlette takes a lot more work and turns out to be a more fragile product. And yet, it is one of my most beloved pastries. Made with laminated dough coated in sugar, the arlette starts off as a three-inch (7.5-cm) segment that is delicately stretched with a rolling pin into a ten-inch-(25-cm) long oval. You know it's ready to bake when you can see the clear shadow of your hand behind the dough as you hold it up to the light.

Said to have originated in the south of France, the beautifully caramelised cookie is as thin as a leaf and features concentric rings that look like agate stone. A bit of gentle pressure between your thumb and forefinger, and delicate pieces break off, each buttery bite almost melting on your tongue. My favourite way to eat the arlette is to smash it up on top of ice cream and scoop up the flaky pieces with a spoon as they slightly soften with the melting cream.

I've always wondered why the arlette is so little known, even by pastry chefs in France. The fragility and the resulting inconvenience of the arlette keep it from earning a place next to more mainstream bakery selections. Most bakers opt to make the more user-friendly palmier, which can be up to ten times thicker and at least half again the size. But I love the arlette because it reminds me of an heirloom mechanical watch. The skill and finesse required to make such a beautiful object mean it should be treasured. Fragile can in fact mean precious; challenging can mean rewarding. As I create, I set my own definitions, and I choose to see the brighter side every time.

As a chef, I never have the opportunity to wear watches, since working in the kitchen means keeping one's wrists and hands free of accessories. In my whole life, I have owned just one—an old pocket watch I found in a vintage store. It no longer tells time, but I love the masterful wheels and mechanisms within it. Its new function has an even higher goal—that of inspiration.

7

NEVER RUN
OUT OF IDEAS

I had never spent so much money on a piece of clothing before. The crisp white button-down cost forty francs and, for me, it amounted to many days' worth of salary. I remember unwrapping it carefully and putting it up on a hanger in my closet. It was my first 'adult' shirt, and I imagined myself wearing it for the better, more formal occasions in the future.

When the time finally came, many years later, I slipped my arms through the sleeves of the shirt—still with its label attached—and looked in the mirror. The sleeves were two inches (five centimetres) short of reaching my wrists. In the time that had passed with the shirt hanging protected and untouched in my closet, I had outgrown it.

Saving the best for last is a great concept in theory, but it can lead you to waste that 'best' altogether. This is especially true in the realm of ideas. How many ideas have you hung on to, kept buried in the closet of your mind, too precious to share? We wait for an ideal moment; we give ourselves an eternity to strategise. All the while, we forget there are expiration dates. We are subject to an ever-evolving world. What is new and innovative today may not be tomorrow.

At the bakery, we change our menu every six to eight weeks, which requires that we generate fresh ideas consistently. Of course, it takes a while to get to the really good stuff. When I sit down with my team to plan a new menu, the first couple of suggestions are always fragmented and unspectacular. We shout them out, brainstorming, without much care whether they are chosen or not. It's all part of the warm-up. The hard part is persuading people to release those precious 'best' ideas they keep guarded like the king on a chessboard.

There's a fear that we won't ever come across anything 'as good'. That we'll end up being a one-hit wonder. Have a little faith in yourself. It's not about releasing one idea into the world, but embracing idea generation as a lifestyle. Ideas must be seen, heard, touched and tasted to become real. Let them live; otherwise they are merely ghosts in our heads.

The stories included in this chapter feature some of my newest ideas. I talk about how gingerbread inspired me to build not houses, but pinecones snow-dusted with icing sugar. Believe it or not, some of my best ideas, such as the Chocolate Caviar Tart, came from dreams. I also explore disguising certain desserts by using tools meant for one in another's preparation, and you'll see how when I describe the Apple Marshmallow. And I end with my most recent obsession: finding a way to let customers add the final touch, as is the case with the 'Lime Me Up' Tart.

I once attended a dinner where our host uncorked a bottle of Château Margaux 1978, a Bordeaux wine that was as old as I was. The occasion was nothing worth noting, and it felt a bit wasteful as he topped off my glass. But then I reminded myself: wine should be drunk, chocolates eaten, and new clothing worn. Have confidence that there is always a better future ahead. I raised my glass in a toast. *Cheers,* I thought, as I heard a round of clinks. Here's to never running out of ideas.

GINGERBREAD NEED NOT BE HOUSES

A few blocks away from the complex where I grew up was a construction site, and I walked past it daily on my way to school. In the first few weeks, a wooden frame lay upon the ground. Once the foundations were set, beams were erected and the walls climbed upward until finally it came time for the ceiling to be installed.

For centuries, pastries were constructed in very much the same way. A tart or cake is built upward with cream as 'cement' between the layers of sponge and garnished with an ornament or 'cherry on top'. And this was the way I started to construct last winter's new dessert, which featured gingerbread. I layered thin pieces of chocolate on top of one another with a light ginger-spiced mousse in between to 'glue' the structure together. It was sturdy, but had all the charisma of a brick wall.

We build houses with wood, concrete and nails, but surely we could draw inspiration from other structures for desserts, I thought. I began to notice the way other animals in nature construct their dwellings. How a spiderweb spirals from the centre to the outside. The honeybee hive slowly fills in the space of crevices. And there's magic behind the way nature creates every snowflake.

With Christmas just around the corner, the rest of the team gathered for our little tree-lighting ceremony in the greenhouse behind the bakery. I arrived to see a beautifully lit tree, but I also noticed a singular pinecone ornament on a table nearby. From a distance I had mistaken it for a cake. That became the cornerstone for my idea.

The next day, I piped a soft gingerbread-spiced mousse in a spiral tower. Rather than building my dessert from bottom to top, I carefully placed more than sixty small pieces of chocolate, the size and shape of pinecone scales, around the dessert. A light dusting of icing sugar, and all of a sudden, it looked like a solitary pinecone, covered with snow.

If it were up to most cooks, gingerbread would be built into houses, not pinecones. But why not think like a bee or a spider and take inspiration from Mother Nature? Ants were constructing colonies in the sand long before man sought temporary shelter in a cave. We put into practice a small percentage of what's possible. Entire universes exist within our own, and we are free to borrow as we please.

A TART FROM A DREAM

In our dreams, we can be anyone and anywhere we want to be. We control time, space and the sequence of events. And everything, no matter how outlandish it may seem when we wake, feels completely natural. Dream worlds do not follow the rules of reality, and what takes place there is often improbable. But impossible? That's another question entirely.

I keep a small journal next to my bed, and I jot down ideas from dreams. There are but a few minutes to recall them before they slip from my memory. The Chocolate Caviar Tart came to me in one such dream. In it, I entered a brightly lit banquet room. The clink of glassware rang out above the steady murmur of the guests. Somehow I ended up seated at the table, where a waiter dressed in a black jacket served me an entire tin of caviar. I took a bite. And rather than the salty brine of sturgeon eggs, I tasted chocolate instead. Bite after bite, I plunged my spoon into the tin. When I woke up, I could still feel the chocolate pearls rolling on my tongue.

I realised I could create this same chocolate caviar in real life. It was an elegant technique. I mixed a light chocolate ganache and added gelatin so that when the droplets of the warm mixture hit cold oil, it would

set into perfect spheres. Using a tart shell as the caviar 'tin', I filled the inside with an airy coffee cream and topped it generously with the chocolate pearls. A quenelle of whipped cream sat on top, mimicking the crème fraîche that is traditionally offered as a caviar condiment.

In dreams, you never have to obey the rules of logic. Nobody tells you that something is too expensive or too difficult to do. There are no naysayers. Simply imagine, and it becomes real. Why shouldn't all dreams be the roots from which action should grow? The Wright brothers most certainly dreamt of flying before they constructed an airplane. And despite flight seeming like an 'impossible' quest at first, all it needed was just a bit of work. Let's bring that same mind-set to the kitchen. If we think the way we dream, what wonders could we create?

The Chocolate Caviar Tart was a popular item over the New Year holidays. On New Year's Eve, I brought a large tart as dessert to a friend's gathering. After dinner, I took it to the table and positioned it in front of my place setting so that I could help serve it. It was at that point that I realised I had seen the exact same scene before. It had been a dream and now was a reality.

THE MARSHMALLOW'S DISGUISE

In the Greek myths, the gods from Olympus had a fondness for coming down to earth in disguise. Aphrodite threw on a ragged cape to hide her beauty. Zeus transformed himself into a haggard old man. And when the great heroes came in contact with these camouflaged gods, how they treated them could result in an offer of great help or the curse of epic punishment.

The idea of disguise has always intrigued me. I love the surprise of something unexpected. There's a joy in being outsmarted. And after the intrigue, the final discovery feels like a reward.

Today things are a bit more straightforward. How many times have you had a dessert that ended up tasting different or unexpected compared to how it looked? What you see is what you get.

Just after Valentine's Day, I usually reorganise the kitchen equipment, packing away all the plastic moulds I purchased to build chocolates in different shapes. Last time, when I returned from the storage cupboard, I realised I had missed one.

A small plastic mould in the shape of an apple was left on my desk. *What if I give it another function?* I thought. What if this mould could create a chocolate 'disguise' for another medium? In choosing the perfect foil for the dark, rock-solid chocolate, I selected the white and fluffy marshmallow.

I decided to make an Apple Marshmallow. First, I lightly coated the mold with tempered chocolate to create a shell. After it was set, I filled the interior with tender vanilla marsh-mallow and a liquid caramel core. It looked like an apple, had a shell of chocolate, but was filled with vanilla and caramel. Every bite revealed an unforeseen twist. Each new layer deepened the dessert's character.

When I create something new, I think about the final reveal, but I also think about how my customer reaches that point. It should be a process of discovery. As the saying goes, 'Never judge a book by its cover'. You never know what you'll find on the last page. And creations should captivate you from beginning to end.

A BESPOKE LIME TART

'Nonfat, half-caf, extra foam, extra hot, soy latte,' came the order to the barista at our bakery.

'So it's the usual, then,' she responded, and began to make the drink.

I have always been a single espresso kind of guy. But it amazes me how specific an individual coffee order can be. Even the most complex of requests, although it takes a few seconds to process, can be met. You can get your coffee exactly the way you like it.

It's a natural human instinct to want to personalise. We express ourselves through the clothes we wear, the music we listen to, and even the screen saver we select on our computers and phones. In an ideal world, at the bakery we would be able to customise everything to meet each customer's individual preferences. But on a daily basis there are limits. We have to create based on general opinions. Ingredients like chocolate and caramel, for example, are typically loved and considered safe bets for any pastry chef. They are crowd-pleasers and instantly win a fan base. But once in a while, a consensus is hard to reach.

It was the third time the team had gathered to taste-test the spring lime tart and nobody could agree on the right seasoning. What one person found to be sour, another thought was cloyingly sweet. Some suggested adding a pinch of salt, while others preferred to maintain the lime's purity. The feedback on this simple tart was dramatically polarising.

It felt like a tug-of-war of opinions, and we finally realised that we wouldn't be able to decide on what the flavour intensity should be. Each of the staff had his or her own preferences. And that's when I had a thought: *It's the customer who must ultimately be the one to choose.*

But how could we customise a pastry on the spot? It would be impossible to build it from scratch for each person. The solution came to me one night during dinner at an Italian restaurant, when the waiter asked if anyone preferred to add cheese or pepper to the pasta. I found clarity behind the idea of these finishing touches.

Together, the team and I designed a small groove on the top of the Key lime mousse. A thin piece of white chocolate held within it a mixture of Maldon salt, brown sugar and crushed juniper berries, and to the side, a fresh wedge of lime. The three flavours featured in the tart—sweet, salty and sour—each had its own modifiers, and the customers could adjust to their tastes accordingly. Each person could add the desired amount of the sugar and salt mixture and squeeze the fresh juice of the Key lime to his or her liking.

It was a step in a new direction. One that offered a chance for someone other than the chef to modify a dish. It allowed the customer to participate in the process and to have the final word. Creation as a joint effort is surely to become a way of the future.

RECIPES

A TOAST
BEFORE BAKING

Midnight and everyone else had left the kitchen. The resounding voices and clanking of machinery during the daytime had fallen into absolute silence. All alone in a half-lit basement, I stared at what seemed an insurmountable obstacle: I had to glaze a frozen mousse cake.

The instructions were simple: gently warm up chocolate ganache and pour it over the cake until it formed an even, gleaming coat. No matter how hard I tried, it just didn't work. If the glaze wasn't heated up sufficiently, it would cool upon contact with the frozen mousse and the flow would slow like hardening lava before enveloping the entire cake. If it were heated up too long, the ganache would reduce and thicken, which would also inhibit its ability to smoothly drizzle over the cake. Each one of my attempts resulted in bubbles and ripples. And I knew when my chef surveyed it the next day, I would get reprimanded for the poor results.

So there I was, on my own with a challenge and no further direction on how to overcome it. It was my third night in the kitchen, and I was pulling my hair out for what felt like inescapable defeat. 'I did exactly as I was told,' I said out loud, desperate for some sort of help. The empty room had no answers for me.

For some reason, I turned up the fire and began to heat up the glaze as hot as I could, just under the boiling point. And then I decided to add water to increase its fluidity. I was sure my chef would have seen the method as an abomination. *What have I got to lose?* I thought.

I positioned the frozen cake beneath my steaming-hot, watered-down ganache and poured it over the surface of the cake. I watched as it rolled through each crevice and fell down the sides and through the gaps of the wire rack. I stepped back. The work was pristine. Every corner covered with an even and fluid layer of chocolate ganache.

That night, I broke every rule. And what's more, I realised that it was my duty to break them. If the rules don't work for you, make up new ones that do. When you go through the recipes that follow, you may face an empty kitchen, as I did that night. I won't be there to answer your questions or give pointers. But don't be afraid to try, and to experiment, and to look for an alternative that works for you. You may find that baking things in a hotter oven yields better results for you, or that you like to whisk your ganache with a stick blender. 'Why not?' I'd say. That's the real lesson of cooking and creating.

The night I finished properly glazing my cake, I made myself a cup of hot chocolate from the leftover ganache that I had used as the glaze. Every drop was a celebration. This became my go-to hot chocolate, and it is the very first recipe I will share with you.

A NOTE ON MEASUREMENTS

Before you turn the page, I want to share a few words on measurements. Recipes can list the quantities of ingredients by volume or by weight. In the United States, bakers use measuring cups and spoons to determine volume. Elsewhere, bakers use the metric system to determine weight. I've provided both in this book.

Here's a tip: In the bakery, and in my kitchen at home, I rely on a digital precision scale to measure my ingredients by weight. The quantities can vary if you use a measuring cup or spoon. You can pack a cup of flour tightly or loosely. You can grate a tablespoon of lemon zest roughly or finely. But a precision scale ensures that the quantities are exact. I have tested these recipes with both types of measurements, and the results are always delicious. But I have seen more consistent results when I've weighed my ingredients. So if I could give you one more word of advice as you begin to bake, it would be to invest in a digital precision scale. You can find them wherever cooking supplies are sold, both in stores and online.

A NOTE ON TIMING

I always recommend reading a recipe through once before starting. At the beginning of each recipe, I've included the amount of 'active time'—the time spent measuring, mixing, slicing, chopping, churning, cooking and baking the various components necessary to create these desserts. I have not included 'inactive time'—the time spent resting, chilling or proofing these components. Of course, all of those directions are all included in the recipe itself. I've also written a timeline for recipes that require more than one day to complete, to give a sense of where you're going, and where you've been. I hope you enjoy the journey.

BEGINNER RECIPES

HOT CHOCOLATE

I love making this recipe . . . when I need to take a moment. You'd be surprised how much comfort a mug of hot chocolate can bring.

SKILL LEVEL Beginner

TIME 15 minutes

YIELD 8 to 10 servings

INGREDIENTS

Whole milk	7 cups	1645 grams
Dark chocolate *(53% or higher cocoa content)*, finely chopped	2¼ cups	306 grams
Unsweetened cocoa paste, finely chopped	¼ cup	42 grams
Mini Me's (page 116) or marshmallows (page 121) *(for serving, optional)*	as needed	as needed

1. Bring the milk to a boil in a medium saucepan over low heat.
2. Combine the chocolate and cocoa paste in a medium heatproof bowl. Pour the hot milk over them and let stand for 30 seconds.*
3. Whisk the chocolate, cocoa paste and milk, scraping the bottom of the bowl where the chocolate tends to settle.
4. When the chocolate and cocoa paste have been incorporated into the milk, pour the desired amount into your favourite mug.

* Using different types of chocolate is a good way to customise your own blend of hot chocolate.

SERVING INSTRUCTIONS Serve hot, topped with Mini Me's (page 116) or marshmallows (page 121).

STORAGE INSTRUCTIONS The chocolate milk can be kept in a closed airtight container in the refrigerator for up to 4 days. Stir liberally and reheat over low heat when desired.

CHOCOLATE PECAN COOKIES

I love making this recipe . . . because of its forgiving nature and utterly addictive results.

SKILL LEVEL Beginner

TIME 15 minutes one day before; 20 minutes the day of

YIELD 20 cookies (about 1¾ ounces/50 grams each)

TIMELINE

ONE DAY BEFORE Make dough

THE DAY OF Bake

INGREDIENTS

Dark chocolate chips (*60% cocoa content or greater*)	2 cups	455 grams
Unsalted butter (*84% butterfat*)	3 tablespoons + ½ teaspoon	45 grams
Granulated sugar	1 cup + 2 tablespoons + 2 teaspoons	250 grams
Cornflour (cornstarch)	¼ cup	42 grams
Baking powder	¾ teaspoon	3.75 grams
Kosher salt	½ teaspoon	1 gram
Whole eggs (large), lightly beaten	3 each	3 each (150 grams)
Pecans, coarsely chopped	¼ cup	55 grams

ONE DAY BEFORE

MAKE DOUGH

1. Melt 1½ cups (340 grams) of the chocolate chips (set aside remaining chocolate) in a double boiler: Fill a medium saucepan with about 3 inches (7.5 cm) water and bring it to a simmer. Place the chips in a medium heatproof bowl and place the bowl snugly over the water. Stir slowly with a heatproof spatula to ensure that the chocolate chips are completely melted and smooth before turning off the heat.*

2. Melt the butter in the microwave (about 30 seconds on high). Mix into the melted chocolate with the spatula. Keep warm over the hot water.

3. Combine the sugar, cornflour, baking powder and salt in a large bowl. Add the eggs and whisk until fully blended and the mixture resembles pancake batter. Use the spatula to make sure you incorporate any dry ingredients that have settled on the bottom or sides of the bowl.

4. Slowly whisk in the melted chocolate–butter mixture. (If it has cooled and begun to solidify, gently reheat it before incorporating.)

5. Gently fold in the remaining ½ cup (115 grams) chocolate chips and the pecans with the spatula.±

6. Transfer the dough to a shallow baking dish. Cover with plastic wrap pressed directly onto the surface of the batter, to prevent a skin from forming. Refrigerate overnight to rest.

THE DAY OF

BAKE

1. Place a rack in the centre of the oven and preheat the oven to 375°F (190°C) for conventional or 350°F (175°C) for convection. Line a baking tray with baking paper.

2. Using your hands, break the dough into pieces the size of your palm (about 3½ tablespoons/50 grams). Roll the dough into balls and place them on the baking tray at least 2 inches (5 cm) apart from one another. Press gently on the top of each ball with the palm of your hand to make a thick disk. This dough doesn't spread much, so the disks should be relatively close to the size of cookie you'd like.

3. Bake on the centre rack for 4 minutes. Rotate the tray 180 degrees and bake for about 4 minutes more. When the cookies are just beginning to crack on top but the dough is set on the edge and has a soft spot about the size of a 10-cent coin in the centre, remove from the oven.

4. Let the cookies cool on the tray for 5 to 7 minutes, to further set.

5. Remove the cookies from the tray and set aside. Reline the cooled tray with clean baking paper and continue with the remaining dough.

* If even a drop of water gets into the chocolate, it can seize and turn grainy. Double-check that all equipment is dry and that the bowl covers the rim of the saucepan, well above the water, to avoid any steam.

± It's great to make sure your ingredients are mixed well, but too much mixing overworks the dough and causes it to become tough. That's why many great recipes call for a period for the dough to rest.

SERVING INSTRUCTIONS All cookies are best eaten while warm. A glass of ice-cold milk helps.

STORAGE INSTRUCTIONS The dough can be wrapped in plastic wrap and kept in the refrigerator for 3 days or frozen for up to 1 week. (Thaw in the refrigerator for a few hours before baking.) The baked cookies can be kept in a closed airtight container at room temperature for up to 2 days.

MINI MADELEINES

I love making this recipe . . . because it takes only 5 minutes to bake (faster than boiling water), and even faster to eat!

SKILL LEVEL Beginner
TIME 15 minutes one day before; 15 minutes per batch the day of
YIELD 100 mini madeleines

TIMELINE
ONE DAY BEFORE Make batter
THE DAY OF Pipe, bake and serve

INGREDIENTS

Unsalted butter *(84% butterfat)*	8 tablespoons	115 grams
Dark brown sugar	1 tablespoon	15 grams
Honey	2 teaspoons	15 grams
Granulated sugar	½ cup	100 grams
Kosher salt	½ teaspoon	1 gram
Plain flour, sifted	1 cup	120 grams
Baking powder	½ teaspoon	4 grams
Whole eggs (large), at room temperature	3 each	3 each (150 grams)
Grated lemon zest	½ lemon	½ lemon
Grated orange zest	½ orange	½ orange
Cooking oil spray	as needed	as needed
Icing sugar *(for serving)*	as needed	as needed

SPECIAL TOOLS

Microplane (for grating zests)
Uncut piping bag
Nonstick mini madeleine tin
Small sieve

ONE DAY BEFORE

MAKE BATTER

1. Melt the butter, brown sugar and honey in a medium saucepan over low heat. Stir gently with a heatproof spatula to ensure that nothing burns. Keep the mixture warm over very low heat, or reheat if necessary.*

2. Combine the granulated sugar, salt, flour and baking powder in a large bowl and mix well with a whisk. Form a well in the centre of the dry ingredients and add the eggs one by one, whisking to incorporate each before adding the next.±

3. When the eggs are fully incorporated and the batter is smooth, slowly whisk in the butter mixture. Whisk in the lemon and orange zests. The batter will still be runny and similar in consistency to cake batter. Cover with plastic wrap pressed directly onto the surface of the batter, to prevent a skin from forming. Refrigerate overnight to rest.‡

THE DAY OF

PIPE, BAKE, AND SERVE

1. Place a rack in the centre of the oven and preheat the oven to 375°F (190°C) for conventional or 350°F (175°C) for convection.§

2. Using a rubber spatula, place 2 large scoops of batter in a piping bag so that it is one-third full. Push the batter down toward the tip of the bag.

3. Cut an opening about ½ inch (1.25 cm) straight across the tip of the bag.

4. Hold the cooking oil spray about 4 inches (10 cm) away from a nonstick mini madeleine tray and spray evenly in all the cavities.

5. Holding the piping bag at a 90-degree angle about ½ inch (1.25 cm) above the tray, pipe the madeleine batter into the cavities so that it fills each about three-quarters of the way to the top.

6. Bake the madeleines for 2 to 2½ minutes on the centre rack. When you see the batter puff up in the centre, rotate the tray 180 degrees. Bake for 2 to 2½ minutes more, until the sides of the madeleines are golden blond and the centre has set.

7. Unmould immediately. Bang the corner or sides of the madeleine tray against your work surface so that the fresh madeleines drop out.**

* Using different types of honey is a great way to naturally flavour madeleines. I love acacia and wildflower honeys.

± Use room temperature eggs to avoid cooling down the batter. If the batter is too cold, the butter may congeal when you add it.

‡ Many recipes containing baking powder do well to rest overnight. This helps with rising, which is especially important for the madeleine—a pastry that puffs up in the center when it bakes.

§ In general for baking pastries, set your oven to convection if the option is available. This allows the heat to flow more evenly. It's an ideal setting because it helps pastries bake evenly on all sides.

**If you find that the madeleines stick to the mould, for the next batch, try spraying a bit more cooking oil spray. Also, keeping the mould clean and washing it thoroughly with a soft sponge after use will also prevent the madeleines from sticking.

SERVING INSTRUCTIONS Using a small sieve, sprinkle icing sugar evenly over the freshly baked madeleines. Eat immediately (do not wait more than even a few minutes!).

STORAGE INSTRUCTIONS Madeleines are good only when freshly baked. Do not attempt to store them. However, you can keep the batter in a closed airtight container, with plastic wrap pressed onto the surface, in the refrigerator for up to 3 days.

MINI ME'S

I love making this recipe . . . and finding all the ways I can add a little crunch and texture to other desserts with it.

SKILL LEVEL Beginner
TIME 1 hour 45 minutes
YIELD 200 meringues

INGREDIENTS
SWISS MERINGUE

Icing sugar	2¼ cups	266 grams
Egg whites (large)	4 each	4 each (120 grams)

SUGGESTED FLAVOURINGS

Ground cinnamon	½ teaspoon	1.5 grams
Grated lemon zest	1 lemon	1 lemon
Peppermint extract	1 teaspoon	5 grams

SPECIAL TOOLS

Instant-read thermometer
Uncut piping bag
Ateco #804 plain tip (⅜-inch/
  1 cm diameter)

1. Preheat the oven to 200°F (95°C) for conventional or 175°F (80°C) for convection.

2. Fill a medium saucepan with about 3 inches (about 7.5 cm) of water and bring to a simmer. Combine the icing sugar and egg whites in a medium heatproof bowl (the metal bowl of a stand mixer is fine) and place on top of the saucepan of simmering water. The bowl should sit on the rim of the saucepan, well above the water.

3. Whisk the egg white mixture constantly as it warms. When it reaches 113°F (45°C) and feels hot to the touch, remove from the heat.*

4. Using a stand mixer or hand mixer fitted with a whisk, whip the egg whites on high speed. As they whip, the egg whites will triple in volume, thicken and cool. When finished, the meringue will be very fluffy and hold a medium-stiff peak. This should take about 5 minutes, depending on your mixer.±

5. With a rubber spatula, gently fold the desired flavouring into the meringue. Feel free to separate the meringue into batches and use different flavours. Just make sure you keep all tools clean for each to avoid mixing them.‡

6. Cut the tip of a piping bag to snugly fit a #804 plain tip. Using a spatula, place 2 large scoops of meringue in the bag so that it is one-third full. Push the meringue down toward the tip of the bag.

7. Line a baking tray with baking paper. At each corner, pipe a small dot of meringue under the baking paper and push the paper flat. This will help keep it 'glued' to the baking tray.

8. Holding the piping bag at a 90-degree angle about ½ inch (1.25 cm) above the baking tray, pipe a dot of meringue with steady, even pressure until it reaches the size of a 5-cent coin. Pull the piping bag straight up to create a fine point. (You should have a teardrop-shaped meringue.) Repeat piping drops about ½ inch (1.25 cm) apart until all the meringue is used, refilling the piping bag as necessary. (You might need to use a few baking trays, depending on the size of the Mini Me's.)

9. Bake the meringues for 20 minutes. Rotate the tray 180 degrees and bake for 20 minutes more. Continue to rotate every 20 minutes until the meringues are completely dry, about 1 hour 20 minutes. The Mini Me's should be crispy all the way through.

10. Transfer the Mini Me's, still on the baking paper, to a wire rack to cool completely. When cool, remove gently from the baking paper with your fingers.

* This kind of meringue, in which you dissolve the sugar in the egg whites over heat before you whip them, is known as a 'Swiss meringue'.

± Don't worry about overwhipping the meringue. It won't affect the final outcome of the product, so better to overwhip than underwhip.

　When making meringue, it is very important to use clean tools. If a drop of oil (or other fat) or egg yolk gets into the egg whites, the meringue will not whip properly.

‡ The more you work the meringue, the looser its structure becomes. When it bakes, a loose meringue will become flat and dense. It is very important to be as gentle as possible at this stage.

　When choosing flavourings, pick ones that are very concentrated. Ground spices, alcohol-based extracts, and citrus zests are all good options. You can also add a drop of natural food colouring to your Swiss meringue to create coloured Mini Me's.

SERVING INSTRUCTIONS These are a perfect topping for ice cream, cereal, cookie batter, hot chocolate, cake or fruit.

STORAGE INSTRUCTIONS Mini Me's can be kept in a closed airtight container at room temperature, away from humidity, for up to 1 week. Extra Mini Me's can be used for Christmas Morning Cereal (page 169) or to top your Hot Chocolate (page 110).

POPCORN CHOUQUETTES

I love making this recipe . . . for a portable snack on the run.

SKILL LEVEL Beginner

TIME 1 hour 45 minutes

YIELD About 50

INGREDIENTS

CARAMELISED POPCORN

Popcorn kernels	¼ cup	50 grams
Vegetable oil	1 teaspoon	3 grams
Granulated sugar	½ cup + 1 tablespoon	115 grams
Brown sugar (light or dark)	¼ cup, loosely packed	50 grams
Corn syrup	1 tablespoon	20 grams
Water	1 tablespoon	10 grams
Unsalted butter *(84% butterfat)*	4 tablespoons	56 grams
Bicarbonate of soda	1 teaspoon	2 grams
Kosher salt	1 teaspoon	2 grams

PÂTE À CHOUX

Water	⅓ cup	75 grams
Whole milk	4 tablespoons + 1 teaspoon	68 grams

SPECIAL TOOLS

Candy thermometer

Stand mixer with paddle attachment (optional)

Uncut piping bag

Ateco #803 plain tip (⁵⁄₁₆-inch/0.8 cm diameter)

Pastry brush (optional)

Unsalted butter *(84% butterfat)*	5½ tablespoons	75 grams
Granulated sugar	1 teaspoon	3 grams
Kosher salt	1 teaspoon	2 grams
Plain flour	⅔ cup	98 grams
Whole eggs (large)	3 each	3 each (150 grams)

FINISHING

Egg wash	as needed	as needed
(1 egg and 1 egg yolk, beaten together)		
Pearl sugar	⅓ cup	50 grams

MAKE CARAMELISED POPCORN

1. Line a baking tray with baking paper. Combine the popcorn kernels and vegetable oil in a medium saucepan. Cover with a lid and cook over medium heat until the kernels begin to pop. Vigorously shake the saucepan to prevent the popcorn from burning. Continue to cook until you no longer hear the kernels popping, about 5 minutes. Spread the popcorn on the baking tray to cool. Discard any unpopped kernels.

2. Combine the granulated sugar, brown sugar, corn syrup and water in another medium saucepan and bring to a boil over medium heat. Cook without stirring until the caramel reaches 239°F (115°C) and turns a colour similar to honey.

3. Add the butter to the saucepan and slowly swirl to mix. Cook until the caramel reaches 300°F (149°C) and is about two shades darker and the bubbles are much smaller.

4. Add the bicarbonate of soda and salt. Be careful! The bicarbonate might cause the caramel to splatter. Whisk until completely incorporated.

5. Using a heatproof spatula, fold the popcorn into the caramel until it is well coated. Pour the popcorn back onto the baking tray. Separate the popcorn clusters immediately with the spatula.

6. When cooled, about 10 minutes, use a chef's knife to finely chop the popcorn. Store in an airtight container until needed.

MAKE PÂTE À CHOUX AND CHOUQUETTES

1. Place a rack in the centre of the oven and preheat the oven to 375°F (190°C) for conventional or 350°F (175°C) for convection.

2. Combine the water, milk, butter, sugar and salt in a medium saucepan. Bring to a boil over medium heat.

3. Add the flour and stir with a wooden spoon until the mixture comes together and forms a dough. Continue to stir the dough until it begins to dry and you see a film start to form at the bottom of the saucepan as the result of the dough sticking, 1 to 2 minutes.

4. Transfer the dough to a stand mixer fitted with a paddle. (If you don't

have a mixer, use a heatproof spatula to mix the dough.) Add the eggs one at a time and mix on low speed, making sure each egg is fully incorporated before adding the next. This may seem difficult at first, but eventually the batter will loosen up.★

5. Cut the tip of a piping bag to snugly fit a #803 plain tip. Using a rubber spatula, place 2 large scoops of choux dough in the bag so that it is one-third full. Push the dough down toward the tip of the bag.

6. Line a baking tray with baking paper. Holding the piping bag at a 90-degree angle about ½ inch (1.25 cm) above the tray, pipe dots of choux dough about 1½ inches (4 cm) in diameter, spacing them about 1 inch (3.5 cm) apart. Continue piping until all the choux dough has been used, refilling the piping bag as necessary.

7. Using a pastry brush or the tips of your fingers, lightly brush the egg wash on the choux. Sprinkle the caramelised popcorn over the choux, completely covering the surface. Do the same with the pearl sugar. Using your fingers, press the popcorn and pearl sugar into the choux to ensure that they stick as the choux bake.

8. Bake the choux on the centre rack for 10 minutes. Rotate the tray 180 degrees and bake for 10 minutes more. When finished, the choux will be golden brown and feel light to the touch. When broken open, the choux should be mostly hollow.

9. Let the choux, still on the baking paper, cool. When cool, remove gently from the baking paper with your fingers.

★ When making pâte à choux, the amount of eggs needed will vary. The consistency of the choux dough dictates how many eggs should be added. To check the consistency of the choux dough, dip a rubber spatula into the dough and pull straight up. The dough should form a smooth V-shaped 'ribbon' on the end of the spatula when it's ready.

SERVING INSTRUCTIONS Serve at room temperature. The finished Popcorn Chouquettes are best consumed within 12 hours of baking.

STORAGE INSTRUCTIONS Pâte à choux dough can be kept in a closed airtight container in the refrigerator for up to 4 days. Try making some of the other recipes like Vanilla Religieuse (page 137) and Paris–New York (page 145).

MARSHMALLOW CHICKS

I love making this recipe . . . for the kids and the child within ourselves.

SKILL LEVEL Beginner

TIME 2 hours

YIELD 12 chicks

INGREDIENTS

EGGSHELLS

Whole eggs (large, in white shells)	12 each	12 each
Cooking oil spray	as needed	as needed

SOFT CARAMEL

Pouring cream *(35% milk fat)*	¾ cup	160 grams
Light corn syrup	⅓ cup	100 grams
Dark brown sugar	2 tablespoons	24 grams
Granulated sugar	¼ cup	51 grams
Fleur de sel	¼ teaspoon	2 grams

MARSHMALLOW

Powdered gelatine	4 teaspoons	12 grams
Water	½ cup + 2 tablespoons	125 grams
Granulated sugar	1 cup	205 grams
Light corn syrup	⅓ cup	101 grams

SPECIAL TOOLS

Egg scissors

Clean egg carton

Candy thermometer

3 uncut piping bags or 2 uncut bags and 1 baking paper cornet

Stick blender (recommended)

Stand mixer with whisk attachment

Ateco #803 plain tip (5/16-inch/0.8 cm diameter)

| Honey | 2 tablespoons | 32 grams |
| Water | ¼ cup + ½ tablespoon | 75 grams |

ASSEMBLY
| Yellow sanding sugar | ⅓ cup | 60 grams |
| Dark chocolate, finely chopped and tightly packed *(for decoration)* | 1 tablespoon | 10 grams |

PREPARE EGGSHELLS

1. Using egg scissors, remove the narrow point of the eggshells. Make sure to remove any small fragments as you cut. Empty the eggs (you can save the yolks and whites for another recipe or for breakfast the next day). Carefully peel away and discard the inside membrane from the eggshell.

2. Fill a large saucepan halfway with water and bring to a boil over medium heat. Lay out paper towels on the work surface.

3. Gently place the empty eggshells into the boiling water and let them simmer for 1 minute. Carefully remove the shells with a slotted spoon. Place the shells hole down on the paper towels to drain out any excess water. Let the shells cool completely.

4. Lightly coat the inside of the eggshells with cooking oil spray. Rub the spray evenly over the interior of the shells with your finger to make sure the surface is covered. This will help ensure that the marshmallow does not stick to the shell. Reserve the shells in a clean egg carton until ready to fill.*

MAKE SOFT CARAMEL

1. Combine the cream, corn syrup and brown sugar in a small saucepan. Bring to a boil over medium heat. Remove from the heat and set aside, keeping it warm.

2. Place an empty medium saucepan over high heat. When the saucepan is hot, sprinkle a thin, even layer of granulated sugar into the saucepan. As the sugar melts and caramelises, slowly whisk in the rest of the sugar, one small handful at a time, until all the sugar has been added.±

3. When all of the sugar has caramelised and turned deep amber, slowly stream in one-third of the hot cream, whisking constantly. Be careful! The cream might cause the caramel to splatter. When incorporated, whisk in the next third, and then the last.‡ When all of the cream has been added, turn down the heat to low and continue to whisk the caramel until it reaches 221°F (105°C), 4 to 5 minutes. Remove from the heat, whisk in the fleur de sel, pour into a medium heatproof bowl, and let cool completely.

4. When the caramel has cooled, stir well to reemulsify any fat that may have separated. Fill a piping bag with the caramel and refrigerate until needed.

*   Try to avoid getting any cooking oil spray on the outside of the eggshell to keep it clean.

±   This method of cooking sugar is called a 'dry caramel' because it starts with a dry pan and no water. When caramel starts with water, it is called a 'wet caramel'. I prefer the dry version because it allows you more control over the caramelisation.

‡   A whisk will work well here, but if you have a stick blender, using this will re-emulsify the fat quickly and give the caramel a smoother consistency.

MAKE MARSHMALLOW

1. Sprinkle the gelatine over the water in a small bowl. Stir and let sit for about 20 minutes to bloom.

2. Combine the granulated sugar, corn syrup, honey and water in a medium saucepan. Bring to a boil over medium heat. Cook without stirring until the syrup reaches 248°F (120°C).§

3. Carefully pour the hot syrup into a stand mixer fitted with a whisk and add the bloomed gelatine. Let it cool for 5 minutes, until warm. Then whip on low speed until combined. Increase the speed to medium–high and continue to whip for 4 to 6 minutes. The mixture will turn white and quadruple in volume. When the marshmallow is firm enough to hold a peak, stop whipping.

4. Cut the tip of a piping bag to snugly fit a #803 plain tip. Using a rubber spatula, place 2 large scoops of marshmallow in the bag so that it is one-third full. Push the marshmallow down toward the tip of the bag. Remove the caramel-filled piping bag from the refrigerator and cut an opening about ½ inch (1.25 cm) wide straight across the tip of the bag.

ASSEMBLE CHICKS

1. Working as quickly as possible, assemble the chicks one at a time. While the marshmallow is still warm, pipe it into an eggshell to fill it three-quarters full. Set the piping bag with marshmallow aside. Pipe a cherry-size dollop of the soft caramel into the centre of the marshmallow. Pick up the marshmallow-filled piping bag and fill the eggshell to the brim. Then, holding the tip ¾ to 1 inch (2 cm) above the egg, pipe a marshmallow teardrop on top, pulling the tip away as you finish. This will form a small beak for the chick.** Immediately sprinkle with yellow sanding sugar to cover all exposed areas of the marshmallow. Continue filling the remaining eggshells one at a time. Refill your piping bag with marshmallow as necessary.±±

2. Melt a small amount of dark chocolate in the microwave. Mix it gently, making sure it is not too hot. Pour the chocolate into the third piping bag or the baking paper cornet and cut a very small opening across the tip, about the size of the tip of a pen. Pipe 2 small dots onto each chick's head for 'eyes'. Let set at room temperature for at least 1 hour before serving.

§ This is the temperature at which sugar reaches the 'soft ball' stage. It will hold a shape without becoming hard and brittle.

** If the marshmallow starts to cool and set, microwave it in the bag for 5 to 10 seconds.

±± If you wait too long to sprinkle the sanding sugar, it will not stick to the marshmallow. Speed is very important at this stage.

SERVING INSTRUCTIONS Serve at room temperature.

STORAGE INSTRUCTIONS Marshmallow chicks can be kept in a closed airtight container at room temperature for up to 1 week. Leftover marshmallow can be spread onto a baking tray and cut into squares for Hot Chocolate (page 110). Leftover caramel can last for 7 days in the refrigerator and be used for Paris–New York (page 145), Apple Marshmallow (page 162), or Chocolate Caviar Tart (page 184).

VANILLA ICE CREAM

GLUTEN
GF
FREE

I love making this recipe . . . at the start of every summer so that I can eat other desserts à la mode throughout the season.

SKILL LEVEL Beginner

TIME 2 hours

YIELD About 1 quart (1 litre); 15 to 20 small scoops

INGREDIENTS

Whole milk	2¼ cups	530 grams
Pouring cream *(35% milk fat)*	¾ cups	169 grams
Vanilla beans *(preferably Tahitian)*, split lengthwise, seeds scraped	2 each	2 each
Granulated sugar	¾ cup	154 grams
Egg yolks (large)	5 each	5 each (100 grams)

SPECIAL TOOLS

Instant-read thermometer
Medium sieve
Ice cream machine

1. Combine the milk, cream and vanilla pods and seeds in a medium saucepan. Start to warm the mixture over low heat.

2. Whisk the sugar and egg yolks together in a medium bowl until fully combined.

3. When the milk mixture reaches 95°F (35°C) or feels just warm to the touch, remove from the heat. Stream one-third into the yolks, whisking constantly until fully blended, to temper the yolks. Whisk the tempered yolks into the remaining warm milk. Return the saucepan to low heat.

4. Whisking constantly, cook the ice cream base over low heat until it reaches 185°F (85°C) or feels very hot to the touch and becomes thick enough to coat the back of a spoon.*

5. Remove from the heat. Strain the ice cream base through a medium sieve into a 1 litre container.

6. Fill a large bowl with ice and water. Place the container of ice cream base in the ice bath. Stir with a whisk every 10 minutes, until chilled. This stops the base from continuing to cook.

7. When the base has cooled, pour it into the ice cream machine and churn according to the manufacturer's instructions.

8. When finished churning, transfer the ice cream to an airtight container. Allow the ice cream to harden in the freezer for at least 1 hour before serving.

* When a custard reaches this consistency, it's called *nappé*, which means 'glazed' in French.

SERVING INSTRUCTIONS I like my vanilla ice cream plain or topped with Mini Me's (page 116)!

STORAGE INSTRUCTIONS Ice cream can be kept in the freezer for up to 1 week.

APPLE TARTE TATIN

I love making this recipe . . . because it's 80 per cent gorgeous, juicy fruit.

SKILL LEVEL Beginner

TIME 20 minutes one day before; 2 hours the day of

YIELD 6 individual 3-inch (7.5 cm) tarts or 1 large 8-inch (20 cm) tart

INGREDIENTS

SABLÉ BRETON COOKIES

Egg yolks (large)	2 each	2 each (40 grams)
Granulated sugar	6½ tablespoons	85 grams
Salted butter *(84% butterfat)*	4½ tablespoons	65 grams
Plain flour	¾ cup	90 grams
Baking powder	1½ teaspoons	5 grams
Kosher salt	½ teaspoon	1 gram

CARAMELISED APPLES

Granulated sugar	⅔ cup	137 grams
Water	¼ cup + 1½ tablespoons	60 grams
Unsalted butter *(84% butterfat)*, cut in small dice	3 tablespoons	35 grams
Gala apples	7 for 6 individual tarts; 8 for a large tart	
Crème fraîche *(for serving, optional)*		

TIMELINE

ONE DAY BEFORE Make dough

THE DAY OF Bake sablé cookies; make caramelised apples; assemble

SPECIAL TOOLS

Stand mixer with whisk and
   paddle attachments

Ruler

Six 3-inch (7.5 cm) round cake
   tins or one 8-inch (20 cm) round
   cake tin

Candy thermometer

Vegetable peeler

Apple corer

MAKE DOUGH

1. Combine the egg yolks and granulated sugar in a stand mixer fitted with a whisk. Whip on high speed for 2 to 3 minutes until the mixture becomes light and fluffy.

2. Soften (but don't melt!) the butter in the microwave. Reduce the mixer speed to low and mix in the butter.

3. Remove the bowl from the mixer. Using a rubber spatula, fold in the flour, baking powder and salt. Mix just until the flour is incorporated, making sure to scrape down the sides of the bowl with a rubber spatula. The dough should be firm yet pliable.

4. On a piece of baking paper, draw a rectangle a little larger than 6 by 9 inches (15 by 23 cm) with a pencil if making individual tarts, or an 8-inch (20 cm) square if making a large tart. Flip the baking paper over on the work surface. Transfer the dough to the centre of the outline. With an offset spatula or your fingers, shape it into a square ¼ inch (6 mm) thick. Cover with another piece of baking paper. Using a rolling pin with steady, even pressure, push the dough from the middle outward to the edges of the outline. When the dough is rolled evenly and fits the outline, place on a baking tray, still between the two pieces of baking paper, and refrigerate overnight to rest.

THE DAY OF

BAKE SABLÉ COOKIES

1. Place a rack in the centre of the oven and preheat the oven to 350°F (175°C) for conventional or 325°F (160°C) for convection. Line a baking tray with baking paper.

2. Remove the sablé dough from the refrigerator and peel off the top layer of baking paper. Using a cake tin as a guide, trace around the rim with a paring knife and cut out 6 individual cookies or 1 large cookie. Remove the excess dough. Transfer the sablé cookies to the baking tray.

3. Bake the sablé cookies on the centre rack for 8 minutes. Rotate the tray 180 degrees and bake for 8 minutes more or until the sablé cookies turn golden brown. The single large cookie might take a little longer. Transfer the sablé cookies, still on the baking paper, to cool.

MAKE CARAMELISED APPLES

1. Place a rack in the centre of the oven and preheat the oven to 350°F (175°C) for conventional or 325°F (160°C) for convection.

2. Combine the granulated sugar and water in a medium saucepan and bring to a boil over medium heat. Cook without stirring until the caramel reaches 350°F (175°C) and turns a dark amber.

3. Whisk the butter into the caramel. Be careful! The butter will foam and

the caramel will rise in the saucepan. Continue to whisk until all the butter has been incorporated and the caramel is smooth.

4. Divide the caramel equally among the cake tins. It should fill each pan about ⅜ inch (1 cm) deep.

5. Peel and core the apples. If making individual tarts, slice 1 apple into 6 segments. Place 1 whole apple into each small tin. Push 1 segment into the centre of each whole apple. For a large tart, place 1 whole apple in the centre of the large tin. Cut 6 apples in half vertically and place the halves, standing up, in a circle around the whole apple. Slice the remaining apple into 6 segments and fill the spaces between apples.

6. Transfer the cake tins to a baking tray and bake on the centre rack for 30 minutes. Remove from the oven and gently press each apple down with an offset spatula. Return the apples to the oven. Repeat this process 3 or 4 more times. When finished, the apples will have lost half of their size and turned a dark amber. A light skin will have formed on top of the apple, which will become the bottom when unmoulded.

7. Let the caramelised apples cool to room temperature, then refrigerate for an hour for the caramel to set and thicken.

ASSEMBLE

1. To unmould the apples, warm the outside and bottom of the tin by placing it directly on the stovetop over medium heat for 30 seconds. (Alternatively, place it in the oven at 350°F [175°C] for 3 minutes.) Using a small offset spatula or a fork, gently pull the apples away from the edge of the mould.

2. Invert each tin and slide the apple onto a sablé cookie. Serve immediately.

SERVING INSTRUCTIONS Serve warm or at room temperature. A dollop of crème fraîche is a great accompaniment.

STORAGE INSTRUCTIONS Assembled tarts should be consumed the day of. Caramelised apples can be kept in a closed airtight container in the refrigerator for 2 days. Sablé Breton cookies can be kept in an airtight container at room temperature for up to 5 days.

THE PURPLE TART

I love making this recipe . . . during the autumn months when gorgeous stone fruits appear in the farmers' markets.

SKILL LEVEL Beginner

TIME 3 hours 15 minutes

YIELD 6 individual tarts

INGREDIENTS

BLACKBERRY PASTRY CREAM

Whole milk	½ cup + 3 tablespoons	146 grams
Blackberries, puréed	1 cup	135 grams
Egg yolks (large)	4 each	4 each (80 grams)
Cornflour (cornstarch)	⅔ cup + 3 tablespoons	60 grams
Granulated sugar	⅓ cup + 2 tablespoons	94 grams
Unsalted butter *(84% butterfat)*, cut in small dice	4 tablespoons	55 grams

POACHED PLUMS AND CURRANTS

Crème de cassis	¼ cup	50 grams
Granulated sugar	1 cup	250 grams
Water	1½ cups + 5 tablespoons	300 grams

SPECIAL TOOLS

Stand mixer with a paddle attachment

Six 3-inch (7.5 cm) tart rings or one 8-inch (20 cm) tart ring*

Uncut piping bag

Small offset spatula (optional)

* If you would like a larger or smaller tart, feel free to use different size tart rings. This recipe also makes 1 large 8-inch (20 cm) tart.

Elderflower liqueur	⅓ cups	80 grams
Plums, peeled	5 or 6	5 or 6
Blackcurrants	2 cups	300 grams

Unsalted butter (84% butterfat), softened	9 tablespoons	127 grams
Icing sugar	½ cup + 2 tablespoons	81 grams
Vanilla beans (preferably Tahitian), split lengthwise, seeds scraped	1 bean	1 bean
Whole egg (large)	1 each	1 each (50 grams)
Plain flour	1¼ cups, plus more as needed for dusting	165 grams, plus more as needed for dusting
Cornflour (cornstarch)	⅓ cup + 1 tablespoon	47 grams
Almond meal	⅓ cup	30 grams
Kosher salt	½ teaspoon	1 gram
Blackberries, whole	12 each	12 each

MAKE PASTRY CREAM

1. Combine the milk and puréed blackberries in a medium saucepan and bring to a simmer over medium heat. Whisk the egg yolks, cornflour and granulated sugar together in a small heatproof bowl.

2. When the milk and berries come to a simmer, remove from the heat. Stream one-third into the egg yolks, whisking constantly until fully blended, to temper them. Whisk the tempered yolks into the hot milk and berries and return the saucepan to medium-low heat. Continue to cook the pastry cream over medium-low heat, whisking constantly. The pastry cream will become very thick, similar to custard, and start to bubble; cook for an additional 3 minutes. Remove from the heat. Whisk in the butter until fully incorporated.

3. Line a baking tray or shallow bowl with plastic wrap. (The more spread out the pastry cream is, the faster it will cool.) Spread the pastry cream on the plastic wrap. Cover the pastry cream with another piece of plastic wrap pressed directly against the surface to prevent a skin from forming. Refrigerate until completely cooled, about 30 minutes.

POACH PLUMS AND BLACKCURRANTS

1. Combine the crème de cassis, granulated sugar, water and elderflower liqueur in a medium saucepan. Bring to a boil over medium heat, then lower the heat to a simmer. Add the plums. Cut a round of baking paper to fit inside the saucepan and make a small hole in the centre of the round; place it on top of the plums to help them steam and poach evenly.

2. When the plums are fork-tender, add the blackcurrants and simmer just until they begin to burst, 1 to 2 minutes.*

3. Remove saucepan from the heat and let cool at room temperature. Keep the plums in the poaching liquid. They will continue to absorb flavour from the liquid as they sit.

MAKE AND BAKE TART SHELL

1. Cream the butter, icing sugar and vanilla bean seeds for 30 seconds on medium speed in a stand mixer fitted with a paddle. Add the egg, scrape down the sides of the bowl with a rubber spatula, and mix on medium speed until smooth.

2. Combine the plain flour, cornflour, almond meal and salt in a medium bowl. With the mixer on low speed, stir in the flour until just combined, about 10 seconds more.

3. Liberally flour the work surface and a rolling pin. Transfer the dough to the work surface and roll it out into a rectangle about ¼ inch (6 mm) thick. Place on a baking tray and loosely cover with plastic wrap. Refrigerate for 30 minutes.

4. Remove the dough from the refrigerator. Using a tart ring as a guide, cut 6 circles 1 inch (2.5 cm) wider than the outside of the ring, so that the dough rounds will be big enough to come up the sides of the rings.

5. Line a baking tray with baking paper and place the tart rings evenly spaced on the tin. Place a dough round on top of each ring. Push down gently with your fingers and press the dough along the inside of the ring. Use a paring knife to trim excess dough hanging over the edge of the ring. Return to the refrigerator to chill for about 30 minutes.

6. While the tart shells are chilling, place a rack in the centre of the oven and preheat the oven to 350°F (175°C) for conventional or 325°F (160°C) for convection.

7. Bake the tart shells on the centre rack for 8 minutes. Rotate the tin 180 degrees and bake for 8 minutes more or until the tart shells are golden brown.

8. Unmould the tart shells while still warm. Let cool completely at room temperature.

ASSEMBLE

1. Whisk the pastry cream until smooth. Transfer the pastry cream to a piping bag and set aside.

2. Remove the plums and blackcurrants from the poaching liquid with a slotted spoon. Drain the fruits on paper towels; they are ready when no more liquid runs from them. Cut the plums in half vertically with

* Poaching time will vary depending on the ripeness of the plums. If the plums are very ripe, after you add them to the poaching liquid you can just cover them and turn off the heat. If the plums are underripe, simmer until tender.

a paring knife. Remove the stones and slice each half into four even wedges. Set aside.

3. Cut an opening about ½ inch (1.25 cm) wide straight across the tip of the piping bag. Pipe a small amount of pastry cream to cover the base of each tart shell. If you have one, use a small offset spatula to level the pastry cream so that it is perfectly flat.

4. Cut the blackberries in half vertically. Arrange the blackberries, plum slices and blackcurrants decoratively on top of the pastry cream so that it is completely covered.±

5. Refrigerate the tarts until you are ready to serve.

± When arranging the fruits, it is important to show as many angles and cross-sections as possible.

SERVING INSTRUCTIONS Serve chilled straight from the refrigerator.

STORAGE INSTRUCTIONS Tarts should be consumed the day they are built. Leftover pastry cream can be kept in a closed airtight container in the refrigerator for up to 2 days. Leftover tart shells can be kept in a closed airtight container at room temperature for up to 2 days.

INTERMEDIATE RECIPES

CANNELÉ DE BORDEAUX

I love making this recipe . . . to showcase skill and patience when creating the perfect 3:00 pm snack.

SKILL LEVEL Intermediate

TIME 20 minutes one day before (plus 45 minutes if using brand-new cannelé moulds); 1 hour 30 minutes the day of

YIELD 10 medium cannelés (about 2¾ ounces/80 grams each)

TIMELINE

ONE DAY BEFORE Season moulds; make batter

THE DAY OF Bake

INGREDIENTS

Beeswax *(for the moulds)*	as needed	as needed
Whole milk	1½ cups	352 grams
Unsalted butter *(84% butterfat)*	3 tablespoons	42 grams
Vanilla bean *(preferably Tahitian)*, split lengthwise, seeds scraped	½ each	½ each
Egg yolks (large)	3 each	3 each (60 grams)
Dark rum	3 tablespoons	38 grams
Plain flour	½ cup + 2 tablespoons	94 grams
Granulated sugar	¾ cup + 2 tablespoons	180 grams
Kosher salt	½ teaspoon	1 gram

SPECIAL TOOLS

10 cannelé moulds 2 inches tall by 2 inches diameter (5 cm tall by 5 cm diameter)

Pastry brush (optional)

Wire rack

Instant-read thermometer (recommended)

PURCHASING, PREPARING AND CARING FOR CANNELÉ MOULDS

- There are several options when picking out cannelé moulds, but I would recommend using copper moulds. Copper conducts heat extremely well and ensures a crispy exterior and moist flan-like interior as the cannelés bake.
- If you are using copper cannelé moulds for the first time, it is important to season them properly. The traditional way is to use beeswax. Preheat the oven to 400°F (205°C) for conventional or 375°F (190°C) for convection. Melt beeswax in the microwave in 30-second intervals. Brush the inside of the moulds with melted wax and place them on a baking tray in the oven for 10 minutes. Remove and invert on a wire rack over a baking tray to let excess wax drain out. When the moulds cool, repeat this process three more times. Seasoning the moulds in this manner ensures that your cannelés will have a shiny and smooth exterior. It also prevents them from sticking to the moulds. Ideally, this process should be repeated each time you bake cannelés, but it can be done every other time after the first five bakes if the cannelés are unmoulding easily.
- Beeswax can generally be found at specialty stores or online at several retailers. It comes in blocks or chips. I recommend chips simply because they are easier to melt; otherwise they are the same.
- Copper cannelé moulds do not need to be washed. To clean, wipe with a dry towel.

ONE DAY BEFORE

SEASON MOULDS

Prepare cannelé moulds in the method described above.

MAKE BATTER

1. Combine the milk, butter and vanilla bean pod and seeds in a medium saucepan. Bring to a simmer over medium heat. Remove from the heat and let cool to about 100°F (38°C), or lukewarm to the touch.*

2. Whisk the egg yolks into the milk mixture. When they have been incorporated, whisk in the rum.

3. Whisk the flour, sugar and salt together in a medium bowl. Whisk in the warm milk one-third at a time, scraping down the sides and bottom of the bowl between additions. Some air bubbles will form, but keep these to a minimum. When finished, the batter will have the consistency of pouring cream.±

4. Strain the batter through a medium sieve into an airtight container. Before closing, cover with plastic wrap pressed directly onto the surface of the batter, to prevent a skin from forming. Press the lid of the airtight container on tightly. Refrigerate overnight to rest the batter.

* Using a thermometer will result in a more consistent final product, but you can also test the temperature of the milk mixture with your finger: too cold and the butter will congeal; too hot and the egg yolks will start to cook.

± Avoid overwhisking the batter since incorporating too much air will result in dry cannelés.

1. Place a rack in the centre of the oven and preheat the oven to 450°F (230°C) for conventional or 425°F (220°C) for convection.

2. Warm the moulds in the oven for 15 minutes before filling. Preheating the moulds helps ensure that the cannelés will have a crunchy, caramelised exterior.

3. Brush the moulds with a thin layer of melted beeswax. (Too much wax will cause the mixture to spill out of the mould during the baking process.) Gently mix the batter to reincorporate ingredients that may have settled overnight. Be careful not to overmix, or you risk incorporating too much air into the batter. The more uniform the batter is, the better the final product will be.

4. Fill each mould to about ¼ inch (6 mm) from the top, about 2¾ ounces (80 grams) of batter each. When the cannelé bakes, it will rise slightly, then sink, so it is important to leave a small space to account for this rise.

5. Place the moulds on a baking tray and bake on the centre rack for 20 minutes. Rotate the pan 180 degrees, reduce the oven temperature to 350°F (175°C) for conventional or 325°F (160°C) for convection, and bake for 35 to 45 minutes more.‡

6. Let the cannelés, still in their moulds, cool for 10 minutes. Turn the cannelé moulds upside down and gently tap the top until the cannelé drops out onto the wire rack. Let cool completely before serving.

‡ Baking times can vary depending on your oven. Keep an eye on the cannelés' colour during their final minutes to ensure they do not over- or underbake. The bottom of the cannelé should turn a deep maple syrup colour when finished.

SERVING INSTRUCTIONS Eat when cooled to room temperature.

STORAGE INSTRUCTIONS A cannelé is best eaten the day it is baked. However, the batter can be kept in a closed airtight container, with plastic wrap pressed directly onto the surface, in the refrigerator for up to 5 days.

VANILLA RELIGIEUSE

I love making this recipe . . . and the best part is decorating it.

SKILL LEVEL Intermediate

TIME 3 hours

YIELD 12 religieuses

INGREDIENTS

Pâte à choux dough (page 118), unbaked	2 batches	2 batches

VANILLA WHIPPED GANACHE

Gelatine sheet (160 bloom)*	1 each	1 each
Vanilla bean	½ each	½ each
Pouring cream *(35% milk fat)*	1½ cups	364 grams
White chocolate chips	½ cup + 2 tablespoons	81 grams

CHOUX CRUST

Unsalted butter *(84% butterfat)*, softened	5 tablespoons + 2 teaspoons	72 grams

SPECIAL TOOLS

Ruler

2-inch (5 cm) ring cutter

1½-inch (4 cm) ring cutter

2 uncut piping bags

Ateco #804 plain tip (⅜-inch/ 1 cm diameter)

Stand mixer with whisk attachment

Ateco #802 plain tip (¼-inch/0.64 cm diameter)

* If you can't find gelatine sheets, use powdered gelatine.

One gelatine sheet = 1 scant teaspoon (2.3 grams) powdered gelatine.

For every teaspoon of gelatine, bloom in 1 tablespoon (15 grams) water.

Light brown sugar, tightly packed	⅓ cup + 2 tablespoons	89 grams
Plain flour	½ cup + 2 tablespoons	89 grams
GLAZE AND DECORATION		
Glazing fondant±	1½ cups	500 grams
Food colouring (optional)	as needed	as needed
Water	as needed	as needed
Decoration of your choice	as needed	as needed

± Glazing fondant is also known as 'fondant icing' or 'pastry fondant'. It is similar to royal icing but remains shiny when it sets.

MAKE GANACHE

1. Soak the gelatine sheet in a bowl of ice water until soft, about 20 minutes. If using powdered gelatine, sprinkle 1 teaspoon (2.3 grams) over 1 tablespoon (15 grams) water in a small bowl, stir, and let sit 20 minutes to bloom.

2. Using a paring knife, slice the vanilla bean in half lengthwise and add the seeds to the cream in a small saucepan. Bring to a boil over medium heat.

3. When the cream reaches a boil, immediately remove the saucepan from the heat. If using a gelatine sheet, squeeze out any excess water. Whisk the bloomed gelatine into the hot cream until the gelatine is dissolved.

4. Place the white chocolate chips in a medium heatproof bowl. Remove the vanilla bean from the hot cream and pour the cream over the chips. Let stand for 30 seconds.

5. Whisk the white chocolate and hot cream until smooth. Cover with plastic wrap pressed directly onto the surface of the ganache, to prevent a skin from forming. Refrigerate to chill while you make the choux.*

MAKE CHOUX CRUST

1. Stir together the butter and brown sugar with a rubber spatula in a small bowl. Blend until there are no longer any streaks of butter. Add the flour and mix until just combined.

2. Place the dough between two pieces of baking paper on the work surface. Using a rolling pin, roll out the dough to a rectangle a little larger than 13 by 6 inches (33 by 15 cm). Transfer the dough, still between the pieces of baking paper, to a half baking tray and freeze until completely firm, about 30 minutes.

3. Cut 12 circles using a 2-inch (5 cm) ring cutter and another 12 circles with a 1½-inch (4 cm) ring cutter. Remove any excess dough. Cover the baking tray loosely with plastic wrap and refrigerate the crust circles until needed.

* Cream whips better when cold, which is why it's important to work with chilled ganache.

MAKE AND BAKE CHOUX CRUST AND DOUGH

1. Make 2 batches of pâte à choux dough, page 118.
2. Cut the tip of a piping bag to snugly fit a #804 plain tip. Using a rubber spatula, place 2 large scoops of pâte à choux dough in the bag so that it is one-third full. Push the dough down toward the tip of the bag.
3. Use the 2-inch (5 cm) ring cutter to trace 12 circles in pencil about 2½ inches (6 cm) apart on a piece of baking paper. Flip the paper over so the choux dough won't come in contact with the pencil marks and place it on a half baking tray. Trace 12 circles on another piece of baking paper with the 1½-inch (4 cm) ring cutter, about 2 inches (5 cm) apart, and flip that baking papert onto a second half baking tray.
4. Holding the piping bag at a 90-degree angle about ⅝ inch (1½ cm) above the tray, fill the outlines with choux dough, pulling the tip up slightly as you pipe to create a slightly domed shape. Repeat until all the outlines on each tray are filled.
5. Place a circle of choux crust on top of each piped choux, matching the sizes. Press down slightly to make sure the crust adheres to the choux. Leave the choux to dry for 30 minutes at room temperature before baking.
6. While the choux are drying, place a rack in the centre of the oven and preheat the oven to 375°F (190°C) for conventional or 350°F (175°C) for convection.
7. Bake the choux on the centre rack for 15 minutes. Rotate the tray 180 degrees and bake for 15 minutes more. When finished, the choux will be golden brown and feel light to the touch; inside, they should be mostly hollow. Let the choux, still on the baking paper, cool completely.

WHIP GANACHE

1. Transfer the ganache to a stand mixer fitted with a whisk. Whip on high speed until stiff peaks form.±
2. Cut the tip of a piping bag to snugly fit a #802 plain tip. Using a rubber spatula, place 2 large scoops of ganache in the bag so that it is one-third full. Push the ganache down toward the tip of the piping bag.

ASSEMBLE

1. Poke the tip of the piping bag filled with ganache into the bottom of a choux and pipe ganache into the choux. When finished, the choux should feel heavy for its size. Fill all the choux and set them aside on a piece of baking paper.
2. Combine the fondant, your choice of food colouring, and a small amount of water in a small heatproof bowl. Fill a small saucepan with about 2 inches (5 cm) water and bring it to a simmer. Place the bowl snugly over the water. Warm the glaze until it reaches body temperature. It should

± Make sure the ganache is cool before you whip.

be fluid—you may need to add a little bit more water to bring it to the correct consistency.

3. To glaze the choux, dip the top one-third of each of the larger choux into the fondant and pull the choux straight up out of the fondant, letting any excess drip off. Turn the choux glazed side up and return it to the baking paper. Repeat this process with the small choux, balancing them on top of the larger choux while the fondant is still warm. Decorate as you see fit. Refrigerate until the fondant is completely set.

SERVING INSTRUCTIONS Let the religieuses sit out for 5 minutes before serving to soften the ganache.

STORAGE INSTRUCTIONS Religieuses can be kept in the refrigerator for up to 24 hours. Leftover pâte à choux can be kept in a closed airtight container in the refrigerator for up to 4 days. Leftover ganache can be kept in a closed airtight container in the refrigerator for 2 days.

COTTON-SOFT CHEESECAKE

I love making this recipe . . . it's cheesecake for people who don't usually like cheesecake.

SKILL LEVEL Intermediate

TIME 2 hours

YIELD 10 individual 3-inch (7.5 cm) cheesecakes or 1 large 8-inch (20 cm) cake

INGREDIENTS

ALMOND BISCUIT

Egg whites (large)	3 each	3 each (90 grams)
Cooking oil spray (optional)	as needed	as needed
Icing sugar	⅓ cup	45 grams
Almond meal	½ cup	45 grams
Whole egg (large)	1 each	1 each (30 grams)
Egg yolk (large)	1 each	1 each (20 grams)
Plain flour, sifted	⅓ cup	36 grams
Granulated sugar	2½ tablespoons	33 grams

CHEESECAKE MOUSSE

Pouring cream *(35% milk fat)*	⅓ cup + 1 tablespoon	85 grams

SPECIAL TOOLS

Silicone baking mat to fit the quarter baking tray (optional)

Ruler (optional)

Stand mixer with whisk attachment

Ten 3-inch (7.5 cm) metal ring moulds*

Whisk

Uncut piping bag

Ateco #805 plain tip (⁷⁄₁₆-inch/ 1.1 cm diameter)

Blowtorch

---

* If you would like a larger or smaller cake, feel free to use different size ring moulds.

Gelatine sheet (160 bloom)*	½ each	½ each
Granulated sugar	⅓ cup + 1 tablespoon	80 grams
Lemon juice	2 tablespoons	26 grams
Whole-milk ricotta cheese	2¼ cups	528 grams
Granulated sugar *(to brûlée)*	as needed	as needed

* If you can't find gelatine sheets, use powdered gelatine.
  One gelatine sheet = 1 scant teaspoon (2.3 grams) powdered gelatine.
  For every teaspoon of gelatine, bloom in 1 tablespoon (15 grams) water.

MAKE ALMOND BISCUIT

1. Place a rack in the centre of the oven and preheat the oven to 380°F (195°C) for conventional or 355°F (180°C) for convection. Line a quarter baking tray with a silicone baking mat or baking paper.*

2. Combine the icing sugar, almond meal and whole egg in a stand mixer fitted with a whisk. Beat on low speed until combined, scraping the sides and bottom of the bowl with a rubber spatula. Turn the speed to high and mix for 1 minute more. The batter will become pale yellow and fluffy.

3. Remove the bowl from the mixer. Using the rubber spatula, fold in the egg yolk. When the yolk is completely incorporated, carefully fold in the plain flour. Overmixing the batter at this stage will result in a tough biscuit. Transfer the batter to a medium bowl.

4. Wash and dry the mixer bowl and whisk, making sure they are clean and free of any residue. Place the egg whites in the mixer bowl. Whip the egg whites on medium speed until frothy. With the mixer still on medium, slowly stream in one-third of the granulated sugar and continue to whip until the sugar is incorporated. Whip in the remaining sugar in two additions.±

5. With the rubber spatula, fold one-third of the meringue into the batter. Once incorporated, add the remaining meringue, folding gently to avoid deflating the batter. When finished, the batter will be cream-coloured, and you will see bubbles on its surface.

6. Pour the batter onto the middle of the quarter baking tray. Using the spatula, spread the batter to fill the pan. (If you are using a larger baking tray, spread it to fill the outline of the rectangle.) Overworking the batter at this point will result in a tough biscuit. Try to spread the batter as quickly and evenly as possible. When finished, the biscuit should be about ½ inch (1.25 cm) thick.

7. Bake the biscuit on the centre rack for 5 minutes. Rotate the tray 180 degrees and bake for 5 minutes more. When finished, the biscuit will be light brown and will spring back when touched in the centre.

* If you do not have a quarter baking tray, draw a rectangle 10 by 8 inches (25 by 20 cm) on a piece of baking paper in pencil, flip the paper over, and use it to line a larger tray.
  Spraying a light coat of cooking oil spray on the baking tray and then placing the baking paper over it is a good way to 'glue' the paper in place.

± By adding the sugar in stages, you ensure that the sugar will dissolve completely and the meringue will retain as much volume as possible. When finished, the meringue will be light and fluffy and hold a soft peak.

8. Let the biscuit, still on the baking paper, cool completely.

9. Invert onto another piece of baking paper and carefully peel off the original baking paper. Using a 3-inch (7.5 cm) ring mould as a guide, cut 10 circles of biscuit just slightly smaller than the ring mould. Cover with plastic wrap and set aside until needed.[‡]

MAKE CHEESECAKE MOUSSE

1. Whisk the cream in a medium bowl until it doubles in volume and holds a stiff peak. Cover with plastic wrap and refrigerate until needed.[§]

2. Soak the gelatine sheet in a bowl of ice water until soft, about 20 minutes. If using powdered gelatine, sprinkle ½ teaspoon (1.5 grams) gelatine over 1½ teaspoons (7.5 grams) water in a small bowl, stir, and let sit 20 minutes to bloom. Squeeze any excess water out of the gelatine sheet.[**]

3. Combine the sugar and lemon juice in a medium saucepan. Bring to a boil over medium heat to fully dissolve the sugar. Remove from the heat and add the bloomed gelatine. Whisk until the gelatine is fully dissolved. Set the syrup aside, keeping it warm.

4. Gently whisk the ricotta in another medium bowl to break up any large lumps. Slowly whisk the warm lemon syrup into the ricotta until fully blended.

5. With the rubber spatula, gently fold one-third of the whipped cream into the ricotta so as not to deflate the cream. Fold in the remaining two-thirds of the whipped cream. When finished, the cheesecake mixture will have a uniform consistency similar to yoghsurt.

6. Cut the tip of a piping bag to snugly fit a #805 plain tip. Twist the bottom of the bag around the tip to prevent the cheesecake mousse from spilling out. Using a rubber spatula, place 2 large scoops of cheesecake mousse in the bag so that it is one-third full.

ASSEMBLE AND BRÛLÉE

1. Line the baking tray with baking paper. Place ten 3-inch (7.5 cm) ring moulds on the baking tray. Place a circle of almond biscuit in the centre of each mould. Holding the piping bag about 1 inch (2.5 cm) above the centre of the almond biscuit, pipe in the cheesecake mousse to fill the mould. When it is filled to the top, slowly lift the piping bag away while still piping. This will help give the cheesecake a dome-like top. Repeat until all the moulds are filled. Freeze until completely solid, 2 to 3 hours.

2. Remove the cheesecakes from the freezer. Warm the moulds by rubbing your hands around the sides until the cheesecakes slide out. Put them all back in the freezer for a few minutes. Take only one or two out of the freezer at a time and place the unmoulded cheesecakes on a wire rack or a baking tray.[±±]

‡ Don't worry if you can't cut 10 full circles in the biscuits. Use the scraps to create the tenth base; the cheesecake mousse will hold the biscuit together when frozen.

§ Whipped cream will remain stable for up to 1 hour. After that it starts to separate and needs to be whipped again.

** Make sure to squeeze out excess moisture from the gelatine sheet. Otherwise, you risk adding moisture to the cheesecake, which will result in a softer-than-desired consistency.

±± If the cheesecake mousse is not cold enough, it will melt as you brûlée the sugar. Check to make sure it's completely frozen before using the blowtorch.

3. Sprinkle a thin, even layer of granulated sugar on top of a cheesecake. Holding the blowtorch about 1 inch (2.5 cm) away from the cake, caramelise the sugar with a focused, high flame (this is very similar to making crème brûlée). When the first layer of sugar is completely caramelised, sprinkle 2 teaspoons (10 g) more granulated sugar on the caramelised surface and brûlée again. Repeat this step one more time for a total of three layers. Repeat with the remaining cheesecakes.‡‡

4. When all the cheesecakes have been brûléed, place them in the refrigerator to thaw completely, 2 to 3 hours.

‡‡By layering the sugar in this way, you create a caramelised surface that can stay crunchy even after several hours in the refrigerator.

When caramelising the sugar, it is important to work quickly to prevent the cheesecake from melting.

SERVING INSTRUCTIONS Serve directly from the refrigerator.

STORAGE INSTRUCTIONS The cheesecakes should be consumed within 24 hours of thawing. Unbrûléed cheesecakes can be kept in the freezer, wrapped well, for up to 1 week.

PARIS–NEW YORK

I love making this recipe . . . as my go-to crowd-pleaser because the combination of peanut butter, chocolate and caramel appeals to almost everyone.

SKILL LEVEL Intermediate

TIME 2 hours 30 minutes one day before; 1 hour 45 minutes the day of

YIELD 6 individual pastries

INGREDIENTS

DARK CHOCOLATE MOUSSE

Gelatine sheet (160 bloom)*	½ each	½ each
Pouring cream *(35% milk fat)*	½ cup	112 grams
Whole milk	⅓ cup	78 grams
Dark chocolate *(70% cocoa content)*, finely chopped	⅓ cup + 2 tablespoons	77 grams

PEANUT BUTTER CREAM

Gelatine sheet (160 bloom)*	½ each	½ each
White chocolate, finely chopped	¼ cup	34 grams
Smooth peanut butter	¼ cup	60 grams

* If you can't find gelatine sheets, use powdered gelatine.
One gelatine sheet = 1 scant teaspoon (2.3 grams) powdered gelatine.
For every teaspoon of gelatine, bloom in 1 tablespoon (15 grams) water.

TIMELINE

ONE DAY BEFORE Make mousse, cream, soft caramel, and caramelised peanuts

THE DAY OF Make and bake choux; make caramel glaze; assemble

SPECIAL TOOLS

Stand mixer with whisk attachment

Instant-read thermometer

Candy thermometer

Stick blender (recommended)

4 uncut piping bags

Ateco #869 open star tip (⅜-inch/1 cm diameter)

2¾-inch (7 cm) ring cutter

3 Ateco #804 plain tips (⅜-inch/1 cm diameter; a few sizes up or down is fine)

Pouring cream *(35% milk fat)*	½ cup + 2 tablespoons	150 grams

Pouring cream *(35% milk fat)*	7 tablespoons	105 grams
Dark brown sugar	1 tablespoon	12 grams
Granulated sugar	2 tablespoons	25 grams

CARAMELIZED PEANUTS
Granulated sugar	2 tablespoons	25 grams
Water	1 tablespoon	10 grams
Peanuts, unsalted	½ cup	63 grams
Icing sugar	1 teaspoon	5 grams
Ground cinnamon	½ teaspoon	1 gram
Kosher salt	½ teaspoon	1 gram

Pâte à choux dough (page 118), unbaked	2 batches	2 batches

CARAMEL GLAZE
Glazing fondant±	½ cup	200 grams
Soft caramel (from above)	¼ cup	60 grams

± Glazing fondant is also known as 'fondant icing' or 'pastry fondant'. It is similar to royal icing but remains shiny when it sets.

ONE DAY BEFORE

MAKE MOUSSE

1. Soak the gelatine sheet in a bowl of ice water until soft, about 20 minutes. If using powdered gelatine, sprinkle ½ teaspoon (1.5 grams) gelatine over 1½ teaspoons (7.5 grams) water in a small bowl, stir, and let sit 20 minutes to bloom.

2. Whip the cream in a stand mixer fitted with a whisk until it forms medium-stiff peaks. Transfer to a medium bowl, cover with plastic wrap, and refrigerate until needed.

3. Bring the milk to a boil in a small saucepan over medium heat. Remove from the heat.

4. If using a gelatine sheet, squeeze out any excess water. Whisk the bloomed gelatine into the hot milk until the gelatine is dissolved.

5. Place the dark chocolate in a medium heatproof bowl. Pour the hot milk over the chocolate and let it stand for 30 seconds.

6. Whisk the chocolate and milk until smooth. When finished, the ganache should have the consistency of mayonnaise. Let the ganache cool to 100°F (38°C).*

7. Using a rubber spatula, fold one-third of the whipped cream into the ganache until just combined. Fold the remaining two-thirds of the

* At this temperature, the ganache will remain smooth but won't melt the whipped cream.

cream into the ganache until all the cream has been incorporated, folding gently so as not to deflate the cream by overmixing.

8. Cover with plastic wrap pressed directly on the surface of the mousse, to prevent a skin from forming. Refrigerate for at least 12 hours to set.

MAKE CREAM

1. Soak the gelatine sheet in a bowl of ice water until soft, about 20 minutes. If using powdered gelatine, sprinkle ½ teaspoon (1.5 grams) gelatine over 1½ teaspoons (7.5 grams) water in a small bowl, stir, and let sit 20 minutes to bloom.

2. Combine the white chocolate and peanut butter in a small bowl.

3. Bring the cream to a boil in a small saucepan over medium heat. Remove from the heat. If using a gelatine sheet, squeeze out any excess water. Whisk the bloomed gelatine into the hot cream until the gelatine is dissolved.

4. Pour the hot cream over the white chocolate and peanut butter and let stand for 30 seconds.

5. Whisk the white chocolate, peanut butter and hot cream until homogeneous and smooth. When finished, the peanut butter cream will have a very loose consistency; it will continue to set overnight. Cover with plastic wrap pressed directly on the surface of the cream, to prevent a skin from forming. Refrigerate for at least 12 hours to set.

MAKE SOFT CARAMEL

1. Combine 5 tablespoons plus 1 teaspoon (80 grams) of the cream and the brown sugar in a small saucepan. Bring to a boil over medium heat. Remove from the heat and keep warm.

2. Place an empty medium saucepan over high heat. When the saucepan is hot, sprinkle a thin, even layer of granulated sugar into the saucepan. As the sugar melts and caramelises, slowly whisk in the rest of the sugar, one small handful at a time, until all the sugar has been added.

3. When all of the sugar has caramelised and turned light amber in colour, slowly stream in one-third of the hot cream, whisking constantly. Be careful! The cream might cause the caramel to splatter. When incorporated, whisk in the next third, and then the last. When all of the cream has been added, turn down the heat to low and continue to cook the caramel until it reaches 221°F (105°C), 4 to 5 minutes. Pour into a medium heatproof bowl and let cool completely.

4. When the caramel has cooled, whisk in the remaining 1 tablespoon plus 2 teaspoons (25 grams) thin (pouring) cream. Cover with plastic wrap and refrigerate until needed.±

± If the caramel starts to separate, use a stick blender to quickly reemulsify it.

MAKE CARAMELISED PEANUTS

1. Line a baking tray with baking paper.
2. Combine the granulated sugar and water in a medium saucepan. Bring to a boil over medium heat.
3. Meanwhile, in a medium bowl, toss the peanuts with the icing sugar to completely coat.
4. Continue to cook the granulated sugar until it reaches 248°F (120°C). Add the peanuts and stir to completely coat in the syrup.
5. Turn the heat to low. Continue to stir until the sugar crystallises on the outside of the peanuts, about 1 minute.
6. Remove the peanuts from the heat and add the cinnamon and salt. Stir to coat the peanuts. Pour out onto the baking tray and let cool completely. When cooled, store in an airtight container.

THE DAY OF

MAKE AND BAKE CHOUX

1. Make 2 batches of pâte à choux dough, page 118.
2. Place a rack in the centre of the oven and preheat the oven to 375°F (190°C) for conventional or 350°F (175°C) for convection.
3. Cut the tip of a piping bag to snugly fit a #869 open star tip. Using a rubber spatula, place 2 large scoops of choux dough in the bag so that it is one-third full. Push the dough down toward the tip of the bag.[‡]
4. Use a 2¾-inch (7 cm) ring cutter to trace 6 circles in pencil about 2½ inches (6 cm) apart on the baking paper. Flip the paper over so choux dough won't come in contact with the pencil marks and place it on a half baking tray.
5. Holding the piping bag at a 90-degree angle about ⅝ inch (1½ cm) above the tray, use the outlined circles as your guide to pipe 6 even circles about ¾ inch (2 cm) thick.
6. Bake the choux on the centre rack for 15 minutes. Rotate the tray 180 degrees and bake for 15 minutes more. When finished, the choux will be golden brown and feel light to the touch; inside, the choux should be mostly hollow.
7. Let the choux, still on the baking paper, cool completely before filling.

MAKE CARAMEL GLAZE

1. Combine the fondant and ¼ cup (60 grams) of the soft caramel in a small bowl. Warm in the microwave on high power in 20-second intervals, stirring between intervals. When finished the fondant should be slightly warm, 95° to 100°F (35° to 38°C), and just fluid enough to fall back in flat ribbons into the bowl.[§]
2. Cover with plastic wrap pressed directly onto the surface of the fondant, to prevent a skin from forming, and set aside.

[‡] Using a star tip adds extra grooves to the tops of the baked choux, which allows them to hold glaze with ease.

[§] When warming the fondant, it is important not to overheat it. The fondant should only be slightly warm to the touch. Overheating the fondant will cause it to turn dull and to crack when it sets. If the fondant is too thick, add a few drops of water to thin it out.

ASSEMBLE

1. To glaze the choux, dip the top one-third of a choux into the caramel fondant and pull straight up out of the fondant, letting any excess drip off. Turn the choux glazed side up, return to the baking tray, and let the glaze set for about 5 minutes. You can use your fingers to help spread the glaze evenly over the top and sweep off any glaze that may be dripping. Repeat for all the choux.**

2. When the glaze is set, use a serrated knife to gently slice the choux in half horizontally. Place the bottom halves, cut side up, on a piece of baking paper on the work surface.

3. Cut the tips of 3 piping bags to snugly fit a #804 plain tip. Using a clean rubber spatula for each, place 2 large scoops of soft caramel, chocolate mousse and peanut butter cream in separate bags so that each bag is one-third full.

4. Holding the piping bag of caramel at a 90-degree angle about ½ inch (1.25 cm) above the choux, pipe a circle of caramel to cover the entire top of the choux circle.

5. Holding the piping bag of chocolate mousse at a 90-degree angle about ½ inch (1.25 cm) above the caramel, pipe 5 or 6 large teardrops spaced evenly around each circle. Pipe large teardrops of the peanut butter cream between the drops of chocolate mousse.

6. Cover with the glazed tops of the choux shells and press down slightly.

7. Decorate the top of each Paris–New York with caramelised peanuts. Refrigerate before serving.

**As you dip, the fondant will cool. Rewarm the fondant in the microwave in 5-second intervals as needed.

When dipped, place the choux in the refrigerator to set the fondant more quickly.

SERVING INSTRUCTIONS Let the pastry sit out for 5 minutes to temper before serving.

STORAGE INSTRUCTIONS Consume within 24 hours of building. Leftover mousse can be kept in a closed airtight container in the refrigerator for 2 days; peanut butter cream in a closed airtight container in the refrigerator for 2 days; soft caramel in a closed airtight container in the refrigerator for 5 days; caramelised peanuts in a closed airtight container at room temperature for weeks; and pâte à choux in a closed airtight container in the refrigerator for up to 4 days.

PERFECT LITTLE EGG SANDWICH

I love making this recipe . . . for a savoury breakfast. It's something I never get tired of.

SKILL LEVEL Intermediate

TIME 20 minutes one day before; 2 hours 30 minutes the day of

YIELD 12 to 15 sandwiches

INGREDIENTS

BRIOCHE

Strong flour	2½ cups, plus more as needed for dusting	305 grams, plus more as needed for dusting
Kosher salt	1 teaspoon	2 grams
Granulated sugar	3 tablespoons	38 grams
Instant yeast *(preferably SAF Gold Label)**	2 teaspoons	5 grams
Whole eggs (large)	4 each	4 each (200 grams)
Whole milk	1 tablespoon	15 grams
Unsalted butter *(84% butterfat)*, cold, cut into small dice	13 tablespoons	183 grams

TIMELINE

ONE DAY BEFORE Begin brioche

THE DAY OF Shape and bake brioche; bake scrambled eggs; assemble

SPECIAL TOOLS

Stand mixer with dough hook attachment

Pastry brush

Rimmed quarter baking tray

---

* Instant yeast is often used for doughs with higher sugar content, because this yeast needs less water to react and sugar tends to pull water from dough. You can substitute the same quantity of active dry yeast, but you may get a denser final product.

Egg wash *(2 eggs, 1 pinch salt, and a dash of milk, beaten together)*	as needed	as needed
BAKED SCRAMBLED EGGS		
Unsalted butter *(84% butterfat)*	3½ tablespoons	50 grams
Spring onions, medium diced	3 each	3 each
Chives, finely chopped	¼ bunch	¼ bunch
Whole eggs (large)	19 each	19 each (950 grams)
Whole milk	2½ cups	588 grams
Kosher salt	2 teaspoons	5 grams
Freshly ground black pepper	½ teaspoon	1 gram
Gruyère cheese, thinly sliced	12 to 15 slices	12 to 15 slices

ONE DAY BEFORE

BEGIN BRIOCHE

1. Combine the strong flour, salt, sugar, yeast and eggs in a stand mixer fitted with a dough hook. Mix on low speed until the dough forms a ball. Slowly pour in the milk and mix on low until combined. Increase the speed to medium-high for 8 to 10 minutes more to develop the gluten, which will help the dough hold its structure. It should pull off the sides of the bowl cleanly when it's ready.[*]

2. When the dough has reached full gluten development, add the butter, keeping the mixer on medium-high speed. Mix just until the butter is incorporated. The finished dough will be smooth, shiny and deep yellow.[±]

3. Lightly grease a medium bowl with cooking oil spray. Transfer the dough to the bowl and cover with plastic wrap pressed directly onto the surface, to prevent a skin from forming. Proof the dough at room temperature until doubled in size, about 1 hour 30 minutes.[‡]

4. Remove the plastic wrap and punch down the dough by folding the edges into the centre, releasing as much gas as possible. This will help stop the fermentation process. Cover the dough again with plastic wrap pressed directly onto the surface. Refrigerate overnight.

THE DAY OF

SHAPE AND BAKE BRIOCHE

1. Lightly dust the work surface with flour. Place the dough on the work surface. Using a knife, divide the dough into pieces about the size of a golf ball (1¾ ounces/50 grams each).

2. Using the palm of your hand and moderate pressure, press down on the dough and move your hand in a circular motion to tighten the ball. (Think of the motion they do in *Karate Kid* for 'wax on, wax off'.) When

[*] A good way to check if dough is ready is called the 'windowpane test'. Take a small piece of dough and roll it into a ball, then slowly stretch the dough out from the centre. If the gluten is fully developed, you should be able to stretch the dough into a thin, translucent sheet. If the dough tears, it's not quite ready. Mix for a minute or two more and try the windowpane test again.

[±] When making brioche, it is very important that the dough does not overheat. If it does, the butter will start to melt and leak out, which will result in a dry finished product.

[‡] When proofing dough at home, sometimes the kitchen can be too warm (especially when there's other cooking happening). Try to find a spot to proof where the room temperature is not above 75°F (24°C).

finished, you should have a roll no bigger than your palm, with a smooth surface.§

3. Line a baking tray with baking paper. Place the rolls on the tray about 4 inches (10 cm) apart. Lightly drape a piece of plastic wrap over the rolls. Place the pan in a warm spot and proof until doubled in size, about 2 hours.**

4. While the dough is rising, place a rack in the centre of the oven and preheat the oven to 375°F (190°C) for conventional or 350°F (175°C) for convection.

5. When the rolls have doubled in size, lightly brush them with egg wash, making sure the dough is completely coated.

6. Bake the rolls on the centre rack for about 5 minutes. Rotate the tray 180 degrees and bake for 5 minutes more. When finished, the rolls will be golden brown and light for their size.

7. Let the rolls, still on the baking paper, cool completely.

BAKE SCRAMBLED EGGS

1. If the oven was turned off, place a rack in the centre of the oven and preheat the oven to 325°F (160°C) for conventional or 300°F (150°C) for convection. Line a rimmed quarter baking tray with baking paper, letting the paper hang over the sides of the pan. (This allows you to lift the eggs out of the pan after baking.)

2. Melt the butter in a medium sauté pan. Add the diced spring onion and cook over low heat until they become translucent and tender. Take your time and let them caramelise slowly. Spread the spring onion evenly over the prepared baking tray. Sprinkle the chives over the spring onion.

3. Whisk the eggs, milk, salt and pepper together in a medium bowl until thoroughly combined. Pour the eggs into the baking tray. They should come about 1 inch (2.5 cm) up the sides of the tray. Bake the eggs on the centre rack for 12 minutes. Rotate the tray 180 degrees and bake for 12 minutes more, until the eggs spring back when pushed in the centre.

4. Let the eggs, still in the tray, cool at room temperature for 15 minutes.

5. Remove the eggs from the tray by lifting up the baking paper overhang. Invert the eggs onto a cutting board and peel away the baking paper. Using a chef's knife, cut the eggs into 2-inch (5 cm) squares.

ASSEMBLE

1. If the oven was turned off, place a rack in the centre of the oven and preheat the oven to 325°F (160°C) for conventional or 300°F (150°C) for convection.

2. Using a serrated knife, slice each roll in half horizontally. Place the bottom halves of the rolls on a baking tray, place a square of baked

§ Rolling the dough this way helps improve the structure of the brioche and gives the roll a smooth exterior.

** Here's a good way to test whether dough is fully proofed: stick your finger into the center of the roll. The indentation should fill in slowly.

scrambled egg on each, and top with a slice of Gruyère. Bake on the centre rack of the oven until the cheese melts, about 4 minutes.

3. Remove from the oven and add the top of the roll. Serve immediately.

SERVING INSTRUCTIONS Serve warm and fresh out of the oven.

STORAGE INSTRUCTIONS Eat the assembled sandwich immediately. The cooked eggs can be kept in the refrigerator, wrapped in plastic, for up to 2 days. Brioche can be kept in a closed airtight container at room temperature for up to 2 days.

BLACK AND BLUE PAVLOVA

GLUTEN
GF
FREE

I love making this recipe . . . as a chic daytime dessert that is light-as-air and never overwhelming.

SKILL LEVEL Intermediate

TIME 1 hour 30 minutes one day before; 2 hours the day of

YIELD 6 pavlovas

INGREDIENTS

LEMON GANACHE

Gelatine sheet (160 bloom)*	2 each	2 each
Pouring cream *(35% milk fat)*	¾ cup + 2 tablespoons	188 grams
Grated lemon zest	1 lemon	1 lemon
Granulated sugar	¼ cup	51 grams
White chocolate, finely chopped	¾ cup	117 grams
Lemon juice	½ cup + 1 tablespoon	141 grams

* If you can't find gelatine sheets, use powdered gelatine.
  One gelatine sheet = 1 scant teaspoon (2.3 grams) powdered gelatine.
  For every teaspoon of gelatine, bloom in 1 tablespoon (15 grams) water.

TIMELINE

ONE DAY BEFORE Make ganache and compote

THE DAY OF Whip ganache; make meringues; assemble

SPECIAL TOOLS

Microplane

Small sieve (for sifting icing sugar)

Candy thermometer

Stand mixer with whisk attachment

3 uncut piping bags

Ateco #809 plain tip (¹¹⁄₁₆-inch/ 1.75 cm diameter)

3-inch (7.5 cm) ring cutter

Blueberries	2 cups	300 grams
Granulated sugar	¾ cup + 1 tablespoon + 1 teaspoon	171 grams
Powdered pectin	2 teaspoons	3.5 grams
Grated lemon zest	1 lemon	1 lemon
Lemon juice	½ teaspoon	2 grams

BLUEBERRY MERINGUE SHELLS

Egg whites (large)	7 each	7 each (210 grams)
Granulated sugar	1 cup + 2 tablespoons	203 grams
Icing sugar, sifted	1¾ cups	200 grams
Blueberry extract	2 drops	2 drops
Violet food colouring, gel	2 drops	2 drops
Blackberries	42 each	42 each
Icing sugar	as needed	as needed

ONE DAY BEFORE

MAKE GANACHE

1. Soak the gelatine sheets in a bowl of ice water until soft, about 20 minutes. If using powdered gelatine, sprinkle 2 teaspoons (6 grams) gelatine over 2 tablespoons (30 grams) water in a small bowl, stir, and let sit 20 minutes to bloom.

2. Combine the cream, lemon zest and granulated sugar in a small saucepan. Bring to a boil over medium heat. Remove from the heat.

3. If using gelatine sheets, squeeze out any excess water. Whisk the bloomed gelatine into the hot cream until the gelatine is dissolved.

4. Place the white chocolate in a large heatproof bowl. Pour one-third of the hot cream over the chocolate. Let stand for 30 seconds.

5. Whisk the white chocolate and hot cream until incorporated. Add the remaining hot cream and whisk until smooth.

6. Set the ganache aside to cool. When it reaches room temperature, whisk in the lemon juice. Cover with plastic wrap pressed directly onto the surface of the ganache, to prevent a skin from forming. Refrigerate overnight to set.

MAKE COMPOTE

1. Bring about two-thirds of the blueberries to a simmer in a small saucepan over medium heat. Slowly whisk in 1 tablespoon plus 1 teaspoon (14 grams) of the sugar and the pectin and bring to a boil over medium heat.*

* Reserving some fresh blueberries to add at the end will ensure you get some nice chunks of blueberries in the compote.

After adding the pectin, it is important to keep the compote at a boil, while whisking constantly. A drop in temperature will affect how the pectin sets.

2. Slowly stream in the remaining ¾ cup (145 grams) sugar, whisking, and keeping the compote at a boil. Cook until the compote reaches 221°F (105°C) and thickens to a jam-like consistency.

3. Stir in the lemon zest, lemon juice and the remaining blueberries. Remove from the heat and transfer to a small bowl. Cover with plastic wrap pressed directly onto the surface of the compote, to prevent a skin from forming. Refrigerate until completely cooled, at least 45 minutes.

4. Transfer the compote to a piping bag. Refrigerate until needed.

THE DAY OF

WHIP GANACHE

Transfer the lemon ganache to a stand mixer fitted with a whisk. Whip on high speed until it holds a medium-stiff peak, 2 to 3 minutes. Using a rubber spatula, place 2 large scoops of ganache in a piping bag so that it is one-third full. Push the ganache down toward the tip of the bag. Refrigerate until needed.±

MAKE MERINGUES

1. Place a rack in the centre of the oven and preheat the oven to 185°F (85°C) for a conventional oven or 160°F (70°C) for convection.

2. Wash and dry the mixer bowl and whisk, making sure they are clean and free of any residue. Whip the egg whites on medium speed in a stand mixer fitted with a whisk until frothy. Slowly stream in the granulated sugar in three additions, making sure the sugar is dissolved between additions. Continue to whip the egg whites until they form stiff peaks, 2 to 3 minutes.‡

3. Remove the bowl from the mixer and using a rubber spatula, gently fold in the icing sugar in three additions, until completely incorporated. Add the blueberry extract and violet food colouring and continue to fold until the colour is uniform. Be careful not to overwork the meringue, or it will lose volume and become soft.

4. Cut the tip of a piping bag to snugly fit a #809 plain tip. Using a rubber spatula, place 2 large scoops of meringue in the bag so that it is one-third full. Push the meringue down toward the tip of the bag.

5. Line a half baking tray with baking paper. Use a 3-inch (7.5 cm) ring cutter to trace 12 circles in pencil about 2 inches (5 cm) apart on the baking paper. Flip the paper over so the meringue won't come in contact with the pencil marks. At each corner, pipe a small dot of meringue under the baking paper and push the paper flat. This will help keep it 'glued' to the baking tray.

6. Holding the piping bag at a 90-degree angle about 1 inch (2.5 cm) above the baking tray, pipe with steady, even pressure until the meringue fills

± Whipped ganache will generally hold for 1 day, but the texture will change the second day, so it is always better to whip just what you need.

‡ This type of meringue, where you don't heat the sugar, is called a 'French meringue'.

the guideline. Pull the piping bag straight up to create a fine point. You should have a meringue shaped like a big teardrop. Repeat with the remaining guidelines.

7. Bake the shells on the centre rack for 25 minutes. The shells will not be baked through yet. Remove the shells from the oven and gently peel them from the baking paper with your hands. If the shells do not release from the paper easily, return to the oven to bake for 10 more minutes. Place the shells on a piece of baking paper on the work surface.

8. With the flat bottom of the shell facing up, scoop out the inside with a spoon, leaving a thin dome of meringue about ⅜ inch (1 cm) thick. Repeat with the remaining shells.

9. Return the shells to the baking tray with the hollowed-out side down and bake for an additional 30 minutes or until completely dry on the inside. Let them cool completely at room temperature.

10. Using a microplane, sand the peaks off half of the shells to make a flat surface. These will become the bases of the pavlovas. Reserve all the shells in an airtight container until needed.

ASSEMBLE

1. Arrange the bases so that the cavity is facing up. Cut an opening about ½ inch (1.25 cm) wide straight across the tip of the piping bag filled with lemon ganache. Pipe a large dollop of lemon ganache (about 20 grams or 1½ tablespoons) to fill each base.

2. Cut an opening about ½ inch (1.25 cm) wide straight across the tip of the piping bag filled with blueberry compote. (Make sure it's large enough for the whole blueberries.) Pipe about 1 tablespoon (20 grams) of compote onto the centre of the lemon ganache. Continue with the remaining base shells.

3. Arrange 6 or 7 whole blackberries along the edge of each pavlova base. The berries should completely cover the filling.

4. Rest the top shells on the blackberries; if necessary, pipe more lemon ganache on the berries to help the top stick.

5. Using a small sieve, dust each pavlova with icing sugar. Refrigerate until you are ready to serve.

SERVING INSTRUCTIONS Let the pavlovas sit out for 5 minutes to temper before serving.

STORAGE INSTRUCTIONS Pavlovas are best consumed the day they are assembled. They can be stored in the refrigerator for up to 24 hours. Leftover meringues can be stored in a closed airtight container at room temperature for 1 day. Leftover compote and lemon ganache can be stored in the refrigerator for up to 2 days.

PINK CHAMPAGNE MACARONS

I love making this recipe . . . for celebratory occasions requiring a little extra flash and splendour.

SKILL LEVEL Intermediate

TIME 30 minutes two days before; 2 hours 30 minutes one day before; 15 minutes the day of

YIELD 20 to 25 macarons

INGREDIENTS

ROSÉ CHAMPAGNE GANACHE

Water	2 tablespoons	20 grams
Rosé Champagne	¼ cup + 2 tablespoons	96 grams
Unsweetened cocoa powder	1½ tablespoons	9 grams
Pouring cream *(35% milk fat)*	½ cup	115 grams
Egg yolks (large)	3 each	3 each (60 grams)
Granulated sugar	3 tablespoons	38 grams
Dark chocolate *(66% cocoa content)*, finely chopped	1 cup + 1 tablespoon	165 grams

MACARON SHELLS

Almond meal	2 cups	180 grams
Icing sugar, sifted	1¾ cups	203 grams

TIMELINE

TWO DAYS BEFORE Make ganache

ONE DAY BEFORE Make shells; fill and assemble

THE DAY OF Serve

SPECIAL TOOLS

Instant-read thermometer

Candy thermometer

Medium sieve

Food processor (optional)

Stand mixer fitted with whisk attachment

Pastry brush

2 uncut piping bags

Ateco #803 plain tip (5⁄16-inch/ 0.8 cm diameter)

1½-inch (4 cm) ring cutter (optional)

Ateco #804 plain tip (⅜ inch/ 1 cm diameter)

Egg whites (large)	5 each	5 each (150 grams)
Red food colouring, gel	as needed	as needed
Water	2 tablespoons	30 grams
Granulated sugar	¾ cup	154 grams
Gold leaf	25 sheets	25 sheets

TWO DAYS BEFORE

MAKE GANACHE

1. Combine the water, 2 tablespoons (26 grams) of the Champagne, and the cocoa powder in a small bowl. Whisk to make a smooth paste.

2. Combine the pouring cream and the remaining ¼ cup (70 grams) Champagne in a small saucepan. Bring to a boil over medium heat. Remove from the heat.

3. Whisk the egg yolks and granulated sugar together in a second small bowl. Stream one-third of the hot cream and Champagne into the egg yolks, whisking constantly until fully blended, to temper them. Whisk the tempered yolks into the remaining hot cream and Champagne and return the saucepan to medium heat.

4. Continue to cook the custard over medium heat, whisking constantly. The custard will thicken and become a pale yellow. When the custard reaches 185°F (85°C) and is thick enough to coat the back of a spoon, remove it from the heat. Add the cocoa powder paste and whisk until fully incorporated.

5. Place the chocolate in a large heatproof bowl. Strain the custard through a medium sieve over the chocolate. Let stand for 30 seconds.

6. Whisk the custard and chocolate together until smooth, about 30 seconds. When finished, the ganache will have the consistency of mayonnaise. Cover with plastic wrap pressed directly onto the surface of the ganache, to prevent a skin from forming. Refrigerate overnight to set.

ONE DAY BEFORE

MAKE SHELLS

1. Whisk the almond meal and icing sugar together in a medium bowl until there are no lumps.*

2. With a rubber spatula, stir in 3 of the egg whites (90 grams) to create a thick paste. Add red food colouring as needed to turn the base dark pink.±

3. Pour the remaining 2 egg whites (60 grams) into a stand mixer fitted with a whisk. Begin whipping them on medium speed.

4. Combine the water and granulated sugar in a small saucepan. Mix with your hand to create 'wet sand', making sure all the sugar is moistened. Set over medium heat and bring to a boil. Cook the syrup without stirring until it reaches 241°F (116°C).‡

* For an extra smooth finish, I prefer to blend the almond meal and icing sugar together in a food processor. Just be careful not to overwork the almond meal. If you do, it will release oils that will turn the mixture into a paste.

± When adding food colouring to the base, keep in mind that you will mix this into a white meringue, which will lighten the colour by 3 shades or more.

‡ It is important to make sure the inside wall of the saucepan is free of any grains of sugar, which could crystallise and result in a grainy syrup. Use a wet pastry brush to clean the inside of the saucepan as you cook.

5. When the egg whites have tripled in volume and form medium peaks, turn the speed to high and slowly pour the hot syrup down the inside edge of the bowl, making sure to avoid hitting the whisk. When all the syrup has been incorporated, continue to whip on high speed for 1 minute more.§

6. With a rubber spatula, fold one-third of the meringue into the almond meal base. When incorporated, fold in the remaining meringue. Continue to gently fold the macaron batter until all the lumps are gone. The batter should still be slightly warm to the touch.**

7. Cut the tip of a piping bag to snugly fit a #803 plain tip. Using a rubber spatula, place 2 large scoops of macaron batter in the bag so that it is one-third full. Push the batter down toward the tip of the bag.±±

8. Line two half baking trays or one large baking tray with baking paper.‡‡ At each corner, pipe a small dot of batter under the baking paper and push the paper flat. This will help keep it 'glued' to the baking tray.

9. Holding the piping bag at a 90-degree angle about ½ inch (1.25 cm) above the tray, pipe dots of macaron batter 1½ inches (4 cm) in diameter, spacing the macarons at least 2 inches (5 cm) apart.

10. Carefully tap the baking trays by lifting them up a few inches in the air and dropping them flat on the work surface. This will help spread the batter slightly and knock out any air bubbles.

11. Let the macarons air-dry for about 1 hour. A thin skin will form on the macarons so that when they bake they will keep their shape.§§

12. While the macarons are drying, place a rack in the centre of the oven and preheat the oven to 275°F (135°C) for conventional or 250°F (120°C) for convection.

13. Bake the macarons on the centre rack for about 10 minutes. Rotate the tray 180 degrees and bake for 10 minutes more. The macaron shells should be dry and firm to the touch. During the baking process, they will slightly rise from the base and form the signature 'foot'.

14. Let the shells, still on the baking paper, cool completely. Carefully peel them from the baking paper.***

FILL AND ASSEMBLE

1. Match 2 macaron shells that are the same size. Place them flat side up and slightly indent the centre of each shell by gently pressing with your thumb. This will help create a pocket for the ganache. Repeat for all the shells.

2. Using a rubber spatula, work the ganache into a smooth paste.

3. Cut the tip of a piping bag to snugly fit a #804 plain tip. Using a rubber spatula, place 2 large scoops of ganache in the bag so that it is one-third full. Push the ganache down toward the tip of the bag.

4. Holding the piping bag at a 90-degree angle about ½ inch (1.25 cm)

§ How you pour the syrup into the egg whites is very important. Aim for the inside edge of the bowl, where the whisk does not touch. If you pour the syrup onto the whisk, it will splash all over the inside of the bowl and possibly onto your hands. If you pour too fast, you risk cooking the egg whites and deflating the meringue. Slow and steady is the way to go.

** The consistency of the finished batter is very important to the final product. Overworking the batter will result in a flat shell. Underworking the batter will result in a grainy shell.

±± Macaron batter needs to be piped right away, while it's warm, or it will start to set and become clumpy.

‡‡ If piping is not your strong suit, use a 1½-inch (4 cm) ring cutter to trace circles in pencil about 1 inch (2.5 cm) apart on the baking paper. Flip the baking paper over so the batter won't come in contact with the pencil marks.

§§ If the macarons do not dry enough, they will crack and lose their shape when you bake them. It's better to let them dry a few extra minutes if you are unsure if they are ready.

*** If the macarons stick to the paper, place them in the freezer for 15 minutes and they should release much more easily.

above the shell, pipe a large dollop of ganache into the pocket of one half of the shell pair. The ganache should fill the pocket and cover about two-thirds of the surface of the shell.

5. Sandwich the two shells together, pressing until a thin line of ganache is visible all the way around the macaron. Repeat with the remaining shells.

6. Return the filled macarons to the baking tray and cover loosely in plastic wrap. Refrigerate overnight so the macarons can 'age'. They must spend some time in the refrigerator to allow the ganache to slowly soften the shell.±±±

THE DAY OF

SERVE

1. Test to ensure that the outside of the macaron is still crisp but the inside has softened. If the inside is still crisp, rest in the refrigerator for a few hours longer.

2. Lightly dab a drop of water on the top shell with a pastry brush. Using the tip of a paring knife, gently remove a piece of gold leaf and lay it over the macaron.

±±± Depending on the moisture content of the filling, macarons need to age for at least 24 hours in the refrigerator.

SERVING INSTRUCTIONS Enjoy at room temperature.

STORAGE INSTRUCTIONS Filled macarons can be kept in a closed airtight container in the refrigerator for up to 3 days and up to 1 week in the freezer, if frozen immediately after they are filled. Once thawed, they cannot be refrozen.

APPLE MARSHMALLOW

I love making this recipe . . . for all sorts of holidays from Halloween to Christmas to celebrating New York (the Big Apple).

SKILL LEVEL Intermediate

TIME About 4 hours

YIELD 6 Apple Marshmallows

INGREDIENTS

Milk chocolate, finely chopped	2¼ pounds	1 kilogram
Soft caramel (page 121)	2 batches	2 batches

CINNAMON MARSHMALLOW

Gelatine sheet (160 bloom)*	5 each	5 each
Egg whites (large)	3 each (90 grams)	3 each
Granulated sugar	1¼ cups	260 grams
Light corn syrup	3 tablespoons	52 grams
Water	⅓ cup	77 grams

SPECIAL TOOLS

6 plastic apple chocolate moulds, 3 inches (7.6 cm) in diameter and 2¾ inches (7 cm) high

2 palette knives

Wire rack

Stand mixer with whisk attachment

Candy thermometer

2 uncut piping bags

Airbrush

Six 8-inch (20 cm) lollipop sticks

Baking paper cornet

* If you can't find gelatine sheets, use powdered gelatine.
  One gelatine sheet = 1 scant teaspoon (2.3 grams) powdered gelatine.
  For every teaspoon of gelatine, bloom in 1 tablespoon (15 grams) water.

Ground cinnamon	1 teaspoon	2.5 grams
DECORATING		
Red-coloured cocoa butter	1½ cups	200 grams
Marzipan	2 tablespoons	30 grams
Dark chocolate, tightly packed	1 tablespoon	10 grams

MAKE CHOCOLATE SHELLS

1. Melt and temper the milk chocolate (see page 242).
2. Place a wire rack over a baking tray (to catch excess chocolate that drips from the moulds). One at a time, fill the two halves of an apple chocolate mould with the tempered chocolate and let stand for 1 minute. Invert the mould over the wire rack and let the excess chocolate run out of the cavity. As the chocolate sets, use a palette knife to scrape away any excess chocolate on the mould. The chocolate shell should be about the thickness of a credit card. Repeat with the remaining moulds. Refrigerate about 45 minutes to set.
3. To unmould, twist the mould slightly.
4. Reserve the apple shells in a cool place until you're ready to fill them.

MAKE SOFT CARAMEL

Make the soft caramel, page 121. Fill a piping bag with the soft caramel and set aside.

MAKE CINNAMON MARSHMALLOW

1. Soak the gelatine sheets in a bowl of ice water until soft, about 20 minutes. If using powdered gelatine, sprinkle 4 teaspoons (12 grams) gelatine over 5 tablespoons (75 grams) water in a small bowl, stir, and let sit 20 minutes to bloom.
2. Place the egg whites in a stand mixer fitted with a whisk. Begin whipping them on medium speed.*
3. Combine the granulated sugar, corn syrup and water in a medium saucepan. Bring to a boil over medium heat and cook the syrup without stirring until it reaches 266°F (130°C).
4. Remove the syrup from the heat. If using gelatine sheets, squeeze out any excess water. Whisk the bloomed gelatine into the hot syrup until the gelatine is dissolved. Turn the mixer to high speed and slowly pour the hot syrup into the whipped whites, streaming it down the inside of the bowl to avoid hitting the whisk.
5. Continue to whip the marshmallow until almost completely cooled, about 5 minutes. Add the cinnamon and whip until it is incorporated.
6. Using a rubber spatula, place 2 large scoops of cinnamon marshmallow in another piping bag so that it is one-third full. Push the marshmallow down toward the tip of the bag.

* Adding egg whites to marshmallow helps make the final product much lighter and fluffier. Because it will fill a chocolate shell and doesn't need to hold its shape on its own, a softer marshmallow will work well here.

ASSEMBLE

1. While the marshmallow is still warm, cut an opening about ½ inch (1.25 cm) wide straight across the tip of the bag. Starting from the centre of the apple shell, pipe in marshmallow until each half apple shell is three-quarters full. Repeat with remaining halves of the chocolate apple shells.

2. Cut an opening about ½ inch (1.25 cm) wide straight across the tip of the piping bag filled with soft caramel. Place the tip of that bag inside the cinnamon marshmallow and pipe until the marshmallow expands to fill the entire half of the shell. Repeat with the remaining halves of the chocolate apple shells.

3. Fill a medium saucepan with about 2 inches (5 cm) of water and bring to a simmer over medium heat. Place an inverted baking tray over the saucepan to warm. When the baking tray feels warm to the touch, lightly rub the edge of the top half of an apple shell on the surface so that it starts to melt. Repeat with the bottom half of the apple shell. Line up the melted edges of both pieces to glue together. Use your fingers to rub the edges and create a firm seal.

4. Cover the work space where you will be airbrushing the apple shells with baking paper.

5. Melt the red-coloured cocoa butter in a microwave for a few seconds (follow the instructions on the product). Fill your airbrush with the melted cocoa butter and lightly spray the outside of each chocolate apple.

6. Warm a paring knife under hot running water and wipe it dry. Make a small hole in the centre of the top half of the chocolate apple with the knife. Place a lollipop stick through the hole and press it into the marshmallow.

7. To create each 'worm', roll a piece of marzipan into a log. Fill a cornet with a small amount of melted dark chocolate and pipe 2 eyes onto each worm. Place the worms on top of the apples.

SERVING INSTRUCTIONS Serve at room temperature. A fun way to eat the apple is to slice it into segments upon serving.

STORAGE INSTRUCTIONS Apple Marshmallows can be kept in a closed airtight container at room temperature for up to 1 week.

SUNFLOWER TART

I love making this recipe . . . for when I want to add just a bit of je ne sais quoi to the end of a meal.

SKILL LEVEL Intermediate

TIME 3 hours 30 minutes

YIELD 6 individual 3-inch (7.5 cm) cheesecakes or 1 large 8-inch (20 cm) tart

INGREDIENTS

PASSIONFRUIT CURD

Gelatine sheet (160 bloom)*	1 each	1 each
Passionfruit purée	⅓ cup + 2 tablespoons	96 grams
Granulated sugar	½ cup + 2 tablespoons + 1 teaspoon	128 grams
Whole eggs (large)	3 each	3 each (150 grams)
Unsalted butter *(84% butterfat)*, softened	8 tablespoons	112 grams

SPECIAL TOOLS

Instant-read thermometer

Small sieve

Spice grinder

1½-inch (4 cm) silicone half-sphere moulds

Six 3-inch (7.5 cm) tart rings*

Uncut piping bag

* If you would like a larger or smaller tart, feel free to use different size tart rings.

* If you can't find gelatine sheets, use powdered gelatine.
  One gelatine sheet = 1 scant teaspoon (2.3 grams) powdered gelatine.
  For every teaspoon of gelatine, bloom in 1 tablespoon (15 grams) water.

Ground ginger	¼ teaspoon	1 gram
Honey powder	2 tablespoons	15 grams
Saffron threads	½ teaspoon	0.1 gram
Pink peppercorns	1 teaspoon	1 gram
Fennel seeds	1 teaspoon	2 grams

APRICOT COMPOTE

Gelatine sheet (160 bloom)*	3 each	3 each
Fresh apricots, pitted and diced	2 cups (about 6 apricots	400 grams (6 apricots)
Honey	¼ cup	75 grams
Water	¼ cup + ½ tablespoon	50 grams
Spice blend (from above)	2 teaspoons	8 grams
Vanilla sablé tart shell dough (page 130), unbaked	1¾ cups	500 grams
Fresh apricots	6 to 8 each	6 to 8 each
Poppy seeds	½ teaspoon	3 grams

MAKE PASSIONFRUIT CURD

1. Soak all 4 gelatine sheets (for both the passionfruit curd and apricot compote) in a bowl of ice water until soft, about 20 minutes. If using powdered gelatine, sprinkle 1 teaspoon (2.3 grams) gelatine over 1 tablespoon (15 grams) water in one small bowl and 7 teaspoons (15 grams) gelatine over 3 tablespoons (45 grams) water in another small bowl. Stir and let both sit 20 minutes to bloom.

2. Combine the passionfruit purée and 5 tablespoons (64 grams) of the sugar in a medium saucepan. Bring to a boil over medium heat, then remove from the heat.

3. Whisk the eggs and the remaining 5 tablespoons (64 grams) sugar together in a small heatproof bowl. Stream in one-third of the hot passionfruit purée, whisking constantly until fully blended, to temper the eggs. Whisk the tempered eggs into the remaining hot purée. Return the saucepan to medium heat.

4. Whisking constantly, continue to cook the curd over medium heat until it reaches 185°F (85°C). It should be creamy and thick. Remove from the heat.

5. Squeeze the excess water out of 1 gelatine sheet. Add the sheet (or smaller amount of bloomed powdered gelatine) to the curd and whisk until the gelatine is dissolved. Pour the passionfruit curd through a sieve into a medium heatproof bowl.*

6. Let the curd cool to 113°F (45°C), still hot to the touch. Using a whisk,

* For best results, strain the passionfruit curd before cooling.

incorporate the butter until smooth. Cover with plastic wrap pressed directly onto the surface of the curd, to prevent a skin from forming. Refrigerate until set, about 45 minutes.

MAKE SPICE BLEND AND APRICOT COMPOTE

1. Combine all the spices together using a spice grinder and then sift it through a small sieve.
2. Combine the diced apricots, honey and water in a medium saucepan and bring to a simmer over medium heat. Cook until the apricots are soft and a sauce has formed, about 10 minutes.
3. Remove from the heat. Squeeze any excess water out of the remaining 3 gelatine sheets. Add the gelatine sheets (or the remaining bloomed powdered gelatine) and the spice mixture to the apricots and stir until the gelatine is dissolved.
4. Place the silicone half-sphere moulds on a quarter or half baking tray. Portion about 1 tablespoon (20 grams) of the apricot compote into the moulds. Cover loosely with plastic wrap and freeze until hard, 2 to 3 hours.

MAKE AND BAKE TART SHELLS

1. Make the vanilla sablé tart shell dough, page 130.
2. Roll out, cut and fit the dough into six 3-inch (7.5 cm) tart rings. Return to the refrigerator to chill for about 30 minutes.
3. While the tart shells are chilling, place a rack in the centre of the oven and preheat the oven to 350°F (175°C) for conventional or 325°F (160°C) for convection.
4. Bake the tart shells on the centre rack for 8 minutes. Rotate the tray 180 degrees and bake for 8 minutes more or until the tart shells are golden brown.
5. Unmould the tart shells while still warm. Let cool completely at room temperature.

ASSEMBLE

1. Using a rubber spatula, fold the passionfruit curd until it is smooth. Using the spatula, place 2 large scoops of curd in a piping bag so that it is one-third full. Push the curd down toward the tip of the bag.
2. Cut an opening about ½ inch (1.25 cm) wide straight across the tip of the piping bag filled with passionfruit curd. Pipe the curd into each tart shell until it reaches about ¼ inch (6 mm) from the top edge.
3. Unmould the apricot compote domes. Use a paring knife to trim away any rough edges if necessary. Place an apricot dome flat side down in the centre of each tart. Press gently into the curd.
4. Using a paring knife, cut the fresh apricots in half vertically and remove the stones. Slice the apricot halves as thinly as possible (preferably about

the thickness of a credit card). Roll two apricot slices together to create a spiral 'petal'. Place the thinner end of the petal at the edge of an apricot dome. Repeat until the dome is completely surrounded by petals. Repeat for the remaining tarts.

5. Sprinkle poppy seeds on the apricot dome in the centre of the tart so that the dessert resembles a sunflower. Refrigerate until serving.

SERVING INSTRUCTIONS Serve chilled straight from the refrigerator.

STORAGE INSTRUCTIONS The tarts should be consumed the day they are built. Leftover passionfruit curd can be kept in a closed airtight container in the refrigerator for up to 2 days. Leftover tart shells can be kept in a closed airtight container at room temperature for up to 2 days.

CHRISTMAS MORNING CEREAL

I love making this recipe . . . one weekend in early December and eating a bit of it daily until Christmas!

SKILL LEVEL Intermediate

TIME 3 hours

YIELD 6 to 8 servings (about 2 cups/100 grams per serving)

INGREDIENTS

Mini Me's (page 116; use cinnamon for flavouring), baked and cooled	4 cups	400 grams

MILK CHOCOLATE CEREAL

Puffed rice cereal	10 cups	250 grams
Light corn syrup	⅓ cup + 2 tablespoons	117 grams
Granulated sugar	⅓ cup + 2 tablespoons	94 grams
Milk chocolate, finely chopped	1½ cups	250 grams

CARAMELISED HAZELNUTS

Whole blanched hazelnuts	1½ cups	220 grams
Light corn syrup	1 tablespoon	12 grams
Granulated sugar	2 tablespoons	26 grams

SPECIAL TOOLS

3 half-sheet silicone baking mats (optional)

MAKE MINI ME'S

Make Mini Me's, page 116.

MAKE MILK CHOCOLATE CEREAL

1. Place a rack in the centre of the oven and preheat the oven to 365°F (185°C) for conventional or 340°F (170°C) for convection. Line two half baking trays with silicone baking mats or baking paper.

2. Combine the puffed rice and corn syrup in a large bowl. Stir with a rubber spatula and add the sugar until the cereal is evenly coated. Spread the coated cereal in a single layer on the half baking trays.

3. Bake the cereal on the centre rack for 4 minutes. Rotate the pans 180 degrees and bake for 4 minutes more or until golden brown.

4. Let the cereal, still on the baking paper, cool completely. Break the cereal in pieces the size of 5-cent pieces into a clean large bowl. Set aside.

5. Melt two-thirds (1 cup/180 grams) of the milk chocolate in a small bowl in the microwave on high power in 20-second intervals. Stir between intervals with a heatproof spatula to ensure even melting.[*]

6. Add the remaining ½ cup (70 grams) chopped chocolate to the melted chocolate and stir with the spatula until smooth. At this point, the chocolate should be tempered, but double-check by dipping the end of a spoon into the chocolate and letting it set at room temperature. If it sets without streaks, then it is ready. If not, keep stirring and test the chocolate again until it sets with a smooth shine.[±] (See page 242 on tempering.)

7. Pour the tempered milk chocolate over the caramelised cereal. Stir with the spatula until the cereal is evenly coated. Spread the coated cereal in a single layer on the 2 half baking trays. Refrigerate for 2 hours to set.

MAKE CARAMELISED HAZELNUTS

1. Place a rack in the centre of the oven and preheat the oven to 375°F (190°C) for conventional or 350°F (175°C) for convection. Line a half baking tray with a silicone baking mat or baking paper.

2. Combine the hazelnuts and corn syrup in a medium bowl. Stir with a rubber spatula and add the sugar until the hazelnuts are evenly coated. Spread the hazelnuts in a single layer on the lined pan. Bake the hazelnuts on the centre rack for 8 minutes. Rotate the pan 180 degrees and bake for 8 minutes more or until golden brown.

3. Let the hazelnuts, still on the silicone mat, cool completely.

ASSEMBLE

Combine the Mini Me's, milk chocolate cereal and caramelised hazelnuts. Toss well.

[*] To prevent the chocolate from burning you should never heat it in the microwave for more than 30 seconds at a time. Make sure to stir the chocolate between intervals.

[±] This is called 'seeding' because you are adding little pieces of chocolate to the melted chocolate to slowly cool down the temperature. It's a preferred method of tempering when you don't have a large work space.

SERVING INSTRUCTIONS Serve with ice-cold whole milk.

STORAGE INSTRUCTIONS The cereal can be kept in a closed airtight container at room temperature for up to 3 weeks.

'LIME ME UP' TART

I love making this recipe . . . because it offers everyone a chance to add a final touch.

SKILL LEVEL Intermediate

TIME 2 hours 30 minutes one day before; 1 hours 30 minutes the day of

YIELD 6 tarts

INGREDIENTS

LIME MOUSSE

Gelatine sheet (160 bloom)*	2 each	2 each
Pouring cream *(35% milk fat)*	⅓ cup	76 grams
Whole milk	⅓ cup	78 grams
Granulated sugar	2 tablespoons	26 grams
Lime juice	2 tablespoons	40 grams
Grated lime zest	½ lime	½ lime

ITALIAN MERINGUE±

Egg whites (large)	3 each	3 each (90 grams)
Granulated sugar	1 cup	205 grams
Water	2 tablespoons	28 grams

LIME CURD

Gelatine sheet (160 bloom)*	½ each	½ each
Lime juice	¼ cup	48 grams

TIMELINE

ONE DAY BEFORE Make mousse, meringue, lime curd and chocolate décor

THE DAY OF Make and bake tart shell dough; assemble

SPECIAL TOOLS

Stand mixer fitted with a whisk

Candy thermometer

3 uncut piping bags

Acetate or a silicone baking mat

6 rectangular tart moulds, 4¾ by 1½ by ¾ inches (12 by 4 by 2 cm)* or six 2⅝ (6.9 cm) round tart rings*

---

* If you can't find rectangular tart rings, you can substitute 2½-inch (6.5 cm) diameter round tart rings.

171

Grated lime zest	½ lime	½ lime	6 acetate strips, each 12 by ¾ inch (30 by 2 cm)
Granulated sugar	¼ cup + 2 tablespoons	77 grams	Small offset spatula
Whole eggs (large; beat 2 eggs and measure out three-quarters)	4½ tablespoons	1½ each (75 grams)	Medium sieve
Unsalted butter (84% butterfat), softened	4 tablespoons	56 grams	Instant-read thermometer
			2 palette knives
White chocolate chips	1⅓ cups	200 grams	
Vanilla sablé tart shell dough (page 130)	1 cup	250 grams	
Dark brown sugar	1 tablespoon + 1 teaspoon	15 grams	
Maldon salt‡	1 tablespoon + 1 teaspoon	10 grams	
Dried juniper berries, crushed	2 teaspoons	4 grams	
Lime wedges	6 each	6 each	

*   If you can't find gelatine sheets, use powdered gelatine.
    One gelatine sheet = 1 scant teaspoon (2.3 grams) powdered gelatine.
    For every teaspoon of gelatine, bloom in 1 tablespoon (15 grams) water.
±   For most stand mixers, 2½ cups (300 grams) is the smallest amount of Italian meringue that can be made. So for this application you will have to make extra and measure out what you need, ½ cup (30 grams). The remaining meringue can be used for another recipe.
‡   If you can't find Maldon salt, you can use fleur de sel or a flaky sea salt.

ONE DAY BEFORE

BEGIN MOUSSE

1. Soak the gelatine sheets in a bowl of ice water until soft, about 20 minutes. If using powdered gelatine, sprinkle 2 teaspoons (6 grams) gelatine over 2 tablespoons (30 grams) water in a small bowl, stir, and let sit 20 minutes to bloom.

2. Whip the cream in a stand mixer fitted with a whisk until it holds medium-stiff peaks. Transfer the whipped cream to a medium bowl. Cover with plastic wrap and refrigerate.

3. Bring the milk and sugar to a simmer in a small saucepan over medium heat. Remove from the heat.

4. If using gelatine sheets, squeeze out any excess water. Whisk the bloomed gelatine, lime juice and lime zest into the hot milk until the gelatine is dissolved. (After you add the lime juice, the milk will curdle slightly as it reacts to the acid, but keep whisking and it will come back together.) Set aside at room temperature.

MAKE MERINGUE AND FINISH MOUSSE

1. Pour the egg whites into a stand mixer fitted with a whisk. Begin whipping the egg whites on medium speed.

2. Meanwhile, combine the granulated sugar and water in a small saucepan, using your hands to mix until you reach a 'wet sand' consistency. Make sure there are no sugar grains remaining around the edge of the saucepan by wiping the sides of the saucepan with a wet pastry brush. Bring the sugar to a boil over medium heat. Cook the syrup without stirring until it reaches 248°F (120°C), the temperature at which the eggs are cooked and the meringue stabilised. Remove from the heat. By now, the egg whites should hold a soft peak. With the mixer on medium speed, slowly pour the hot syrup down the inside of the bowl to avoid hitting the whisk. Continue whipping the whites until just slightly warm, about 4 minutes.[*]

3. Measure ¼ cup (30 grams) of the meringue into a medium bowl. Add one-third of the lime base to the meringue and gently fold until combined. Add the remaining two-thirds of the lime base and fold it in with a rubber spatula.

4. Using the spatula, fold one-third of the whipped cream into the lime and meringue. When all the cream has been incorporated, add the remaining two-thirds of the whipped cream and continue folding until the cream is completely incorporated.

5. Using the spatula, place 2 large scoops of lime mousse in a piping bag so that it is one-third full.

6. Line a half baking tray with acetate or a silicone baking mat. Place the moulds on the baking tray. Line the moulds with acetate strips.

7. Cut an opening about ½ inch (1.25 cm) wide straight across the tip of the piping bag. Pipe the mousse into the moulds until the mousse reaches just above the edge of the mould. Using a small offset spatula, level the mousse to the height of the mould. Cover loosely with plastic wrap and freeze until set, about 2 hours.

8. One at a time, rub a mould with your hands to gently warm it. Unmould the mousse, still in the acetate strips, back onto the baking tray. Cover with plastic wrap and return to the freezer.

MAKE LIME CURD

1. Soak the gelatine sheet in a bowl of ice water until soft, about 20 minutes. If using powdered gelatine, sprinkle ½ teaspoon (1.5 grams) gelatine over 1½ teaspoons (7.5 grams) water in a small bowl, stir, and let sit 20 minutes to bloom.

2. Whisk the lime juice, lime zest and 2 tablespoons (26 grams) of the granulated sugar together in a medium saucepan and bring to a boil over medium heat. Remove from the heat.

[*] This is called 'Italian meringue'. It is used mostly in fruit mousses and is made with cooked sugar syrup.

3. Whisk the eggs and the remaining 2 tablespoons (33 grams) granulated sugar in a medium heatproof bowl. Stream one-third of the hot lime juice into the eggs, whisking constantly until fully blended, to temper them. Whisk the tempered eggs into the remaining hot juice and return the saucepan to medium heat.

4. Continue to cook the curd over medium heat, whisking constantly, until the curd thickens to a custardy consistency and begins to bubble. Remove from the heat.

5. If using a gelatine sheet, squeeze out any excess water. Whisk the bloomed gelatine into the hot curd until the gelatine is dissolved. Strain the curd through a medium sieve into a medium bowl and set aside to cool.

6. When the curd cools to 113°F (45°C), whisk in the butter until smooth.

7. Cover with plastic wrap pressed directly onto the surface of the curd, to prevent a skin from forming. Refrigerate until set, about 4 hours.

8. Using a rubber spatula, place 2 large scoops of lime curd in a piping bag so that it is one-third full. Push the curd down toward the tip of the bag. Refrigerate until needed.

MAKE CHOCOLATE DÉCOR

1. Melt and temper the white chocolate (see page 242). Transfer the white chocolate to a piping bag.

2. Cut a small hole in the bag (about the size of a dime). Pipe 6 dots of the chocolate, spaced 1½ inches (4 cm) apart, on an acetate sheet. Using a chef's knife at an angle, press the tip of the knife into the chocolate and slowly pull the knife up and away, dragging a 'tail' of white chocolate as you remove the knife. Lay the acetate over a rolling pin to curve the petal. Let set at room temperature for 12 hours before removing the chocolate petals from the acetate.[±]

THE DAY OF

MAKE AND BAKE TART SHELLS

Make the vanilla sablé dough recipe, page 130. Cut to fit the rectangular tart moulds. Bake and unmould. Set aside to cool to room temperature.

ASSEMBLE

1. Combine the brown sugar, salt and crushed juniper berries in a small bowl.

2. Cut an opening about ½ inch (1.25 cm) wide straight across the tip of the piping bag filled with lime curd. Pipe the curd into the tart shells, filling them until the curd just comes over the top edge. Using a small offset spatula, level the curd so that it is the same height as the tart shells.

3. Place the lime mousse on top of the curd in the tart shells. The mousse should be the exact same size as the tart shell. When all the tart shells

± If the petals don't peel off the acetate cleanly, you can place them in the refrigerator for 10 to 15 minutes before unmoulding.

have been filled, place them in the refrigerator to thaw completely, about 1 hour.

4. Using a paring knife, cut ½ inch (1½ cm) off the tip of each mousse to create a ledge. Place a lime wedge where the mousse was cut away.

5. Warm a chef's knife under hot water and cut into the centre of the mousse at an angle along the length of the mousse. Repeat at an opposite angle, creating a small triangle cutaway. This groove will hold the sugar–sea salt–juniper mixture.

6. Fill a white chocolate petal with the sugar–sea salt–juniper mixture and place in the groove in the mousse. Refrigerate until you are ready to serve.

SERVING INSTRUCTIONS Let the tarts sit out for 5 minutes to temper before serving.

STORAGE INSTRUCTIONS Tarts are best if consumed within 24 hours of making. Leftover mousse and lime curd can be kept in closed airtight containers in the refrigerator for 2 days. Leftover tart shells can be kept in a closed airtight container at room temperature for up to 2 days.

FROZEN S'MORES

I love making this recipe . . . on those nights during the winter when it's cold but I still feel like eating ice cream.

SKILL LEVEL Intermediate

TIME 3 hours one day before; 1 hour 30 minutes the day of

YIELD 12 s'mores

TIMELINE

ONE DAY BEFORE Make ice cream; shape ice cream; make chocolate feuilletine

THE DAY OF Begin assembly; make marshmallow; smoke branches; finish assembly and brûlée

---

INGREDIENTS

Vanilla Ice Cream (page 124), freshly churned	1 quart	1 litre
CHOCOLATE FEUILLETINE		
Dark chocolate *(66% cocoa content or greater)*, finely chopped	½ cup	87 grams
Kosher salt	½ teaspoon	1 gram
Feuilletine*	1 cup	94 grams

* If you can't find feuilletine, you can use any kind of crispy wafers or cookies.

SPECIAL TOOLS

2 silicone baking mats

Ruler

12 rectangular ring moulds, 2½ by 1¾ by 1¾ inches (6.5 cm by 4.5 cm by 4.5 cm)

Candy thermometer

Stand mixer with whisk attachment

Uncut piping bag

Small offset spatula

12 wooden branches or sticks, 12 inches (30.5 cm) long

Smoking gun (optional)

Apple wood chips (optional)

Blowtorch

Cooking oil spray	as needed	as needed
MARSHMALLOW		
Powdered gelatine	3 tablespoons	24 grams
Water	⅓ cup + 3 tablespoons	101 grams
Granulated sugar	2 cups	410 grams
Light corn syrup	½ cup + 1 tablespoon	202 grams
Honey	3 tablespoons	65 grams
Water	⅓ cup + 3 tablespoons	101 grams

ONE DAY BEFORE

MAKE ICE CREAM

Make the vanilla ice cream, page 124.

SHAPE ICE CREAM

1. Line a baking tray with a silicone baking mat. Place in the freezer for 30 minutes to chill before using.
2. Using a rubber spatula, spread the just-churned ice cream, which is still relatively soft, on the baking tray into a rectangle about 10 by 8 inches and ¾ inch thick (25 by 20 by 2 cm). Freeze until set, about 4 hours.
3. Invert the ice cream onto a piece of baking paper. Remove the silicone mat and cut twelve 1¼ by 1–inch (2.5 by 2 cm) rectangles of ice cream. Return the rectangles of ice cream to the baking tray, cover with plastic wrap, and reserve in the freezer until needed.*

MAKE CHOCOLATE FEUILLETINE

1. Line another baking tray with baking paper. Melt the dark chocolate in a medium bowl in the microwave on high power in 20-second intervals. Stir with a heatproof spatula between intervals to ensure even melting. When the chocolate is completely melted, stir in the salt. Add the feuilletine and stir until the feuilletine is evenly coated in chocolate. Spread it on the baking tray in an even layer. Refrigerate until set completely.
2. When cold, break up any large pieces of chocolate-coated feuilletine, cover with plastic wrap, and return to the refrigerator until needed.

THE DAY OF

BEGIN ASSEMBLY

1. Coat each rectangle of ice cream in the feuilletine, making sure all sides are covered. Return the coated ice cream to the freezer.
2. Line a baking tray with a silicone baking mat. Place 12 rectangular ring moulds on the baking tray and lightly grease with cooking oil spray.

* After portioning the vanilla ice cream for the frozen s'mores, you will have leftovers. Enjoy a scoop of vanilla ice cream for a snack.

MAKE MARSHMALLOW

1. Sprinkle the gelatine over the water in a small bowl. Stir and let sit for about 20 minutes to bloom.

2. Combine the granulated sugar, corn syrup, honey and water in a medium saucepan and bring to a boil over medium heat. Cook without stirring until the syrup reaches 250°F (121°C).

3. Carefully pour the hot syrup into a stand mixer fitted with a whisk and add the bloomed gelatine. Whip on low speed until the gelatine is completely dissolved. Increase the speed to medium-high and continue to whip for 4 to 6 minutes. The syrup will turn white and quadruple in volume. When the marshmallow is firm enough to hold a medium-stiff peak, stop whipping.±

4. Using a rubber spatula, place 2 large scoops of marshmallow in a piping bag so that it is one-third full. Push the marshmallow down toward the tip of the bag. Cut an opening about 1 inch (2.5 cm) wide straight across the tip of the bag.‡

5. While the marshmallow is still warm, fill each ring mould about three-quarters full. Push a rectangle of ice cream into the centre of the marshmallow in each mould, which will cause the marshmallow to push up and over the sides of the mould. Pipe in a small amount of marshmallow to cover any exposed ice cream. Using a small offset spatula, level the marshmallow so it is the exact height of the mould.§

6. After all the moulds have been filled, let them set quickly for 1 to 2 minutes, then unmould the s'mores by lifting the mould while holding the marshmallow down with your finger. Freeze until set, about 2 hours.

SMOKE BRANCHES OR STICKS (OPTIONAL)

For extra flavour, place the branches or sticks in a sealable plastic bag. Fit the tip of a smoking gun filled with apple wood chips into the bag and seal. Let the smoke fill the bag and close. Set aside for 30 minutes, so the branches or sticks can absorb the smoke.**

FINISH ASSEMBLY AND BRÛLÉE

Remove the s'mores from the freezer and push a branch or stick through each centre. Hold the tip of a blowtorch 3 to 4 inches (7.5 to 10 cm) away from the s'more and brûlée the entire surface of the marshmallow. Serve immediately.

± Speed is very important here. The marshmallow should be used while still hot or it will set very quickly. Make sure you have prepared all the other items needed to assemble the s'mores before starting the marshmallow.

‡ Extra marshmallow can be spread on a baking tray. After it has set, cut it into cubes for hot chocolate.

§ If the marshmallow starts to stiffen and cool, microwave the piping bag for 5 to 10 seconds.

** It's preferable to use a smoking gun outdoors.

SERVING INSTRUCTIONS Serve immediately after toasting.

STORAGE INSTRUCTIONS The frozen s'mores, without sticks, can be kept in a closed airtight container in the freezer for up to 1 week. Leftover feuilletine can be eaten as a snack or sprinkled on top of ice cream. Leftover marshmallow can be kept in a the piping bag for a day and microwaved for a few seconds and then used to make more s'mores.

ARLETTE

I love making this recipe . . . because it is one of the most marvellous of cookies and a sight to behold.

SKILL LEVEL Intermediate
TIME 1 hour 15 minutes one day before; 1 hour the day of
YIELD 8 arlettes

INGREDIENTS

PUFF PASTRY DOUGH

Strong flour	1 cup, plus more as needed for dusting	140 grams, plus more as needed for dusting
Kosher salt	2½ teaspoons	5 grams
White vinegar	½ teaspoon	1 gram
Water, cold	¼ cup + ½ tablespoon	75 grams
Unsalted butter *(84% butterfat)*, softened	4 tablespoons	56 grams

BUTTER BLOCK

Plain flour	⅓ cup + 1 tablespoon	108 grams
Unsalted butter *(84% butterfat)*, softened	8 tablespoons	112 grams

TIMELINE

ONE DAY BEFORE Make dough and butter block; make three folds
THE DAY OF Roll and bake

SPECIAL TOOLS

Stand mixer with dough hook and paddle attachments
Ruler
Large offset spatula

CINNAMON SUGAR

Granulated sugar	2 cups	410 grams
Ground cinnamon	1 tablespoon + 1 teaspoon	10 grams

ONE DAY BEFORE

MAKE DOUGH

1. Combine the strong flour, salt, vinegar, cold water and butter in a stand mixer fitted with a dough hook. Mix on low speed until just blended, about 2½ minutes. The dough should look rough—there's been no gluten development at this stage.[*]

2. Dust the work surface with extra strong flour. With your hands, shape the dough into a 4-inch (10 cm) square about ⅜ inch (1 cm) thick. Cover with plastic wrap and refrigerate until chilled, about 45 minutes.

MAKE BUTTER BLOCK

1. Combine the plain flour and butter in a stand mixer fitted with a paddle. Mix on low speed, scraping down the sides and bottom of the bowl, until there are no streaks of butter. The mixture should still feel like soft butter.

2. Draw a 7-inch (18 cm) square on a piece of baking paper with a pencil. Flip the baking paper over so that the butter won't come in contact with the pencil marks. Place the butter in the centre of the square and spread it evenly with an offset spatula to fill the square. Refrigerate for about 20 minutes, until firm but still pliable.

3. Remove the butter from the refrigerator. It should still be soft enough to bend slightly without cracking. If it is too firm, lightly beat the butter with a rolling pin on a lightly floured work surface until it becomes pliable. Make sure to press the butter back to its original 7-inch (18 cm) square after working it.

4. Arrange the chilled dough in the centre of the butter block so it looks like a diamond in the centre of the square (rotated 45 degrees, with the corners of the dough facing the centre of the butter block sides).

5. Fold the corners of the butter block up and over to the centre of the dough. The butter block should completely cover the dough. Pinch the seams of the butter block together to prevent the dough from peeking through.[±]

MAKE FIRST FOLD

1. Generously flour the work surface and rolling pin. You'll need a rather large work surface for this task. With the rolling pin, using steady, even pressure, roll the butter-covered dough out from the centre so it triples in length. When finished rolling, you should have a rectangle about 12 by 6½ by ¼ inch (30 cm by 16.5 cm by 6 mm).[‡]

[*] Bread flour has more gluten than plain flour. It's ideal for laminated doughs and bread-like doughs that will need to be shaped.

[±] Whenever folding butter, it is important to work swiftly to ensure it doesn't melt.

There are two different types of puff pastry. When the butter is on the inside, it is regular puff pastry. When it is on the outside (as in the case here), it is inverse puff pastry, which can result in a flakier, more caramelised pastry.

[‡] Keeping the shape of the dough is very important at this point to ensure even layers.

2. Place the dough so the longer sides run left to right. From the right side, fold one-third of the dough onto itself, keeping the edges lined up with each other. From the left side, fold one-third of the dough on top of the side that has already been folded. Line up all the edges so that you are left with an even rectangle. The dough is being folded as if it were a piece of paper going into an envelope; this is called a 'letter fold'. Wrap the dough in plastic wrap and refrigerate for 15 to 20 minutes to rest.[§]

§ Resting the dough relaxes the gluten and keeps the butter chilled.

MAKE SECOND AND THIRD FOLDS

1. Remove the dough from the refrigerator. It should be firm but not hard. (If it is not pliable, let it sit briefly to soften.) Place on a lightly floured work surface. With a rolling pin, using steady, even pressure, roll the dough out from the centre vertically from top to bottom. The dough should triple in length and increase in width 1½ times; this will take several passes. When finished, you should again have a rectangle about 12 by 6½ by ¼ inch (30 cm by 16.5 cm by 6 mm).[**]

**When rolling out the dough, it's always best to have the open seams on the top to ensure the layers remain even and don't slide when you are rolling.

2. Rotate the dough so the longer sides run left to right. This time, from the right side fold one-quarter of the dough onto itself. From the left side fold one-quarter of the dough onto itself. The two ends should meet in the middle of the dough. Fold the dough in half where the ends meet. You will have 4 layers of dough on top of one another. This is called a 'double book fold'. Wrap the dough again in plastic wrap and refrigerate for 15 to 20 minutes to rest.

3. Repeat the second (double book) fold again. Wrap the dough in plastic wrap and refrigerate overnight.

THE DAY OF

ROLL AND BAKE

1. Combine the granulated sugar and cinnamon in a small bowl using your hands. Reserve until needed. Line a baking tray with baking paper.

2. Remove the puff pastry from the refrigerator. Place it on a lightly floured work surface. With a rolling pin, using steady, even pressure, roll the dough out from the centre. The dough should triple in length and increase in width 1½ times. This will take several passes. When finished, you should again have a long rectangle about 12 by 6½ by ¼ inch (30 cm by 16.5 cm by 6 mm). Generously sprinkle the dough with ½ cup of cinnamon sugar in an even layer.[±±]

±± Sugar draws out moisture from dough, so once it is added, it is important to work swiftly.

3. Rotate the dough so the longer side runs left to right. Starting at the bottom, roll the dough tightly into a log about 1 inch (2.5 cm) in diameter. Slice the dough into 8 equal segments, each about 1¾ inches (4.5 cm) thick and weighing 1¾ ounces (50 grams).

4. With the spiral facing up on each segment, flatten the dough segments lightly with the palm of your hand until each is a round about 2 inches

(5 cm) in diameter. Place on the baking tray. Refrigerate for 20 minutes to rest.

5. While the dough is resting, place a rack in the centre of the oven and preheat the oven to 375°F (190°C) for conventional or 350°F (175°C) for convection. Invert a half baking tray and place a sheet of baking paper on the flat side.

6. Sprinkle more cinnamon sugar generously on the work surface. Place one of the puff pastry rounds on the cinnamon sugar. With a rolling pin, using steady, even pressure, roll from the centre of the dough up and then down. As the dough sticks to the counter, sprinkle with more cinnamon sugar. Repeat until you have a long oval about 10 inches (25 cm) long and 4 inches (10 cm) wide. The dough should be thin enough to see through it. Gently place the arlette on the baking paper–covered baking tray. Repeat with more dough pieces, leaving 4 inches (10 cm) between arlettes on the baking paper. (Two arlettes should fit on each half baking tray. Keep the remaining dough in the refrigerator.)‡‡

7. Lay a second piece of baking paper on top of the arlettes. Lay a second half baking tray on top of the baking paper, sandwiching the arlettes between the two baking trays.

8. Bake the arlettes on the centre rack for 9 minutes. Rotate the trays 180 degrees and bake 9 minutes more. Remove from the oven and take off the top tray and baking paper. The arlettes should be a deep golden brown. Let the arlettes, still on the baking paper, cool completely.

9. Let the trays cool, then shape and bake the remaining arlettes in the same fashion.

‡‡ Relaxing the dough is a very important part of this process, Make sure to lift the dough off the surface every few passes with the rolling pin, allowing it to contract slightly. This slight relaxation will help with the shape of the final product.

SERVING INSTRUCTIONS Serve at room temperature.

STORAGE INSTRUCTIONS Arlettes should be consumed the day they are baked. Puff pastry dough can be kept in the freezer, wrapped well, for up to 1 week.

ADVANCED RECIPES

CHOCOLATE CAVIAR TART

I love making this recipe . . . and serving it with a sparkling dessert wine.

SKILL LEVEL Advanced

TIME 2 hours 30 minutes one day before; 1 hour 30 minutes the day of

YIELD 6 tarts

INGREDIENTS

WHIPPED COFFEE GANACHE

Gelatine sheet (160 bloom)*	½ each	½ each
Coffee beans	¼ cup	17 grams
Pouring cream *(35% milk fat)*	¾ cup, plus more as needed	190 grams, plus more as needed
White chocolate chips	¼ cup	42 grams
Soft caramel (page 121)	2 batches	2 batches

CHOCOLATE SABLÉ TART SHELL

Unsalted butter *(84% butterfat)*, softened	5 tablespoons	70 grams
Icing sugar	⅓ cup	41 grams
Whole egg (large; beat 1 egg and measure out half)	½ each	½ each (24 grams)
Unsweetened cocoa powder	¼ cup	23 grams

TIMELINE

ONE DAY BEFORE Make ganache, soft caramel, tart shells, and chocolate caviar

THE DAY OF Bake tart shells; make Chantilly cream; assemble

SPECIAL TOOLS

Medium sieve

Instant-read or candy thermometer

Stand mixer with paddle and whisk attachments

3-inch (7.5 cm) ring cutter (optional)

Six 3-inch (9.5 cm) tart rings

Large bowl, at least 4 inches (10 cm) deep

Precision gram scale (optional)

Plastic bottle with drip tip

2 uncut piping bags

Plain flour	½ cup + 1 tablespoon, plus more as needed for dusting	83 grams, plus more as needed for dusting	Small offset spatula
			2⅝-inch (6.9 cm) ring cutter
Kosher salt	1 pinch	1 pinch	
Almond meal	3 tablespoons	17 grams	

CHOCOLATE CAVIAR

Grapeseed oil (*for forming the chocolate caviar*)	7½ cups	1.5 kilograms
Gelatine sheet (160 bloom)*	3½ each	3½ each
Whole milk	½ cup + 1 tablespoon	132 grams
Pouring cream (*35% milk fat*)	¼ cup	58 grams
Granulated sugar	¼ cup	51 grams
Powdered agar	¾ teaspoon	2 grams
Cocoa paste, finely chopped	3 tablespoons	25 grams
Black food colouring, gel	1 teaspoon or as needed	2 grams or as needed

VANILLA CHANTILLY CREAM

Pouring cream (*35% milk fat*)	1 cup	240 grams
Granulated sugar	2 tablespoons	20 grams
Vanilla bean (*preferably Tahitian*), split lengthwise, seeds scraped	½ each	½ each
Gold leaf (optional)	2 sheets	2 sheets

* If you can't find gelatine sheets, use powdered gelatine.
One gelatine sheet = 1 scant teaspoon (2.3 grams) powdered gelatine.
For every teaspoon of gelatine, bloom in 1 tablespoon (15 grams) water.

ONE DAY BEFORE

MAKE GANACHE

1. Soak the gelatine sheets in a bowl of ice water until soft, about 20 minutes. If using powdered gelatine, sprinkle 2 teaspoons (6 grams) gelatine over 2 tablespoons (30 grams) water in a small bowl, stir, and let sit 20 minutes to bloom.

2. Place the coffee beans in a heavy resealable plastic bag. Using a rolling pin, gently crush the beans.

3. Bring the pouring cream to a boil in a small saucepan. Remove from the heat and add the crushed coffee beans. Cover the saucepan with plastic wrap and set it aside to infuse for 15 minutes.

4. Strain the infused cream through a medium sieve into a measuring cup. Add more pouring cream to return it to the original amount. Return the cream to the small saucepan and bring to a boil again over medium heat. Discard coffee beans.

5. Remove the cream from the heat. If using a gelatine sheet, squeeze out any excess water. Whisk the bloomed gelatine into the hot cream until the gelatine is dissolved.

6. Place the white chocolate chips in a small heatproof bowl. Pour the hot cream over the chips and let stand for 30 seconds.

7. Whisk the chips and cream until homogeneous and smooth. Cover with plastic wrap pressed directly onto the surface of the ganache, to prevent a skin from forming. Refrigerate overnight to set.

MAKE SOFT CARAMEL

Make the soft caramel, page 121.

MAKE TART SHELLS

1. Cream the butter and icing sugar on low speed in a stand mixer fitted with a paddle until combined, about 30 seconds. Add the egg and continue to beat until fully blended. Stop the mixer and using a rubber spatula, scrape down the sides of the bowl. Continue to mix until smooth.

2. Combine the cocoa powder, plain flour, salt and almond meal in a medium bowl. Slowly add them to the butter mixture, continuing to mix on low speed until just combined. Scrape down the sides of the bowl and make sure to reach all the way to the bottom, where the dry ingredients may have settled. Mix for 10 seconds more.

3. Using a rubber spatula, remove the dough from the mixer. Form into a flat disk about ¾ inch (2 cm) thick on a sheet of plastic wrap. Wrap well and refrigerate for 30 minutes to firm up.

4. Place the dough on a floured work surface and roll into a rectangle about ⅛ inch (3 mm) thick. Cut the dough with the ring cutter into rounds about ½ inch (1.25 cm) larger than the diameter of the tart rings and place on a sheet of baking paper on a baking tray. Do not stack them. Cover the baking tray with plastic wrap and return the dough to the refrigerator.

MAKE CHOCOLATE CAVIAR

1. Pour the grapeseed oil into a bowl that is at least 4 inches (10 cm) deep. This is important, as the caviar droplets must have enough time to set before settling at the bottom of the bowl. Place the bowl of oil in the freezer for 3 hours before making the chocolate caviar.

2. Soak the gelatine sheets in a bowl of ice water until soft, about 20 minutes. If using powdered gelatine, sprinkle 2 teaspoons (6 grams) gelatine over 2 tablespoons (30 grams) water in a small bowl, stir, and let sit 20 minutes to bloom.

3. Combine the milk and cream in a small saucepan. Bring to a boil over

medium heat. Combine the granulated sugar and agar and slowly whisk into the boiling milk. Lower the heat to a simmer and cook for 4 minutes.*

4. Remove the milk from the heat. If using gelatine sheets, squeeze out any excess water. Whisk the bloomed gelatine into the hot milk until the gelatine is dissolved. Add the cocoa paste and whisk until smooth. Add black food colouring and mix until the chocolate gelée reaches a homogeneous dark colour. Set aside to cool until it reaches between 113° and 122°F (45° and 50°C).±

5. Transfer the chocolate gelée to a plastic bottle with a drip tip.

6. Remove the grapeseed oil from the freezer. Hold the bottle 10 inches (26 cm) above the oil and using a back-and-forth motion, slowly drip the chocolate gelée into the cold oil. As the gelée hits the oil, it will sink and set in a matter of seconds. Since water and oil don't mix, it will form perfect little droplets.‡

7. When all the gelée has been piped into the oil, drain the chocolate caviar in a sieve. Rinse off any extra oil with cold running water. Drain well and transfer to a small container. Refrigerate the chocolate caviar until needed.

THE DAY OF

BAKE TART SHELLS

1. Line a baking tray with baking paper and place the tart rings on the tray. Remove the chocolate sablé circles from the refrigerator. One at a time, slightly warm the dough by pressing it between your hands. The dough needs to be pliable so that it can be pressed into the tart rings without breaking.

2. Centre the circle on top of a tart ring, then slowly push the dough toward the bottom, working your way around the inside of the ring as you go. The dough should fill the tart ring and leave an excess of dough around the edge. Use a paring knife to trim this excess. Return the shells to the refrigerator to chill for 5 minutes.

3. While the shells are chilling, place a rack in the centre of the oven and preheat the oven to 375°F (190°C) for conventional or 350°F (175°C) for convection.

4. Bake the tart shells on the centre rack for 8 minutes. Rotate the tray 180 degrees and bake for 8 minutes more or until dry throughout.§

5. Remove the tart shells from the oven and unmould while still warm. Let cool completely. Reserve in an airtight container until you're ready to fill them.

MAKE CHANTILLY CREAM

Combine the pouring cream, sugar and vanilla bean seeds in a stand mixer fitted with a whisk. Whip until cream triples in volume and holds a medium peak. Cover and refrigerate until needed.

* When using agar, it is very important to be accurate with measurements. I highly suggest using a precision gram scale.

± This temperature will ensure that the gelée sets quickly when it hits the grapeseed oil and isn't too runny.

‡ Try dripping across the entire surface area of the oil, which will give the caviar a chance to set without sticking together.

§ When checking to see if the chocolate shells are baked, rely on the feel of the dough rather than the colour.

ASSEMBLE

1. Transfer the ganache to a stand mixer fitted with a whisk. Whip on high speed until it holds stiff peaks.

2. Using a rubber spatula, place 2 large scoops of ganache into a piping bag so that it is one-third full. Push the ganache down toward the tip of the bag.

3. Fill another piping bag with the soft caramel. Cut an opening about ½ inch (1.25 cm) wide straight across the tip of the bag. Fill the tart shells one-third full with the caramel.

4. Cut an opening about ½ inch (1.25 cm) wide straight across the tip of the piping bag filled with coffee ganache. Pipe the ganache on top of the caramel until it reaches the top rim of the shell. Use a small offset spatula to level the ganache to the height of the tart shell.

5. For a cleaner finish, place a ring cutter the same diameter as the tart shell on top of a shell to act as a mould for the chocolate caviar. Place a spoonful or two of the chocolate caviar on top of the coffee ganache. Gently spread the chocolate caviar to cover the ganache in a thin, even layer. Remove the mould. Continue with the remaining tarts.

6. Remove the Chantilly cream from the refrigerator. Make a quenelle: Warm a small spoon with hot water. Tap it to dry. Drag the spoon through the Chantilly cream until it is filled. Turn the spoon 180 degrees and pull up immediately to make a scoop that is rounded on one end with a narrow tip on the other. Place the quenelle of cream on top of the tart immediately.**

** If you are not confident when it comes to making quenelles, simply place a dollop of vanilla Chantilly cream on the top of the tart for a rustic look. Or use a piping bag to pipe the cream in small teardrops.

SERVING INSTRUCTIONS Let the tart sit out for 5 minutes to temper before serving. For special occasions, place a small piece of gold leaf on top of the chocolate caviar.

STORAGE INSTRUCTIONS The tart should be consumed within 24 hours of making. Leftover caramel can be kept in a closed airtight container in the refrigerator for up to 5 days. Leftover whipped ganache can be kept in a closed airtight container in the refrigerator for 1 day. Leftover chocolate caviar can be kept in a closed container in the refrigerator for up to 2 days and is fun to eat—for example, mixed into iced coffee.

THE ANGRY EGG

I love making this recipe . . . and breaking it apart is even more fun.

SKILL LEVEL Advanced

TIME 5 hours

YIELD 2 eggs

INGREDIENTS

White chocolate, chopped	14 cups	2 kilograms
Fat-soluble red food colouring	3 tablespoons	30 grams
Dark chocolate, chopped	14 cups	2 kilograms
Red-coloured cocoa butter (optional)	as needed	as needed
Truffles, bonbons and other treats	as needed to fill the egg	as needed to fill the egg
Yellow sanding sugar	¼ cup	50 grams

SPECIAL TOOLS

2 egg moulds, 5 by 3½ inches (12.7 by 9 cm)	Wire rack	Precision knife
2 cone moulds with 1-inch (2.5 cm) diameter base, 2 inches (5 cm) high	Instant-read thermometer	Airbrush (optional)
	Two 3-inch (8 cm) round ring moulds	Uncut piping bags or baking paper cornets
2 palette knives	2 acetate sheets, each 8½ by 11 inches (21.7 by 38 cm)	Heat gun
		Cold spray (optional)

MAKE WHITE CHOCOLATE COMPONENTS

1. Melt and temper the white chocolate (see page 242). Place a wire rack over a baking tray to catch excess chocolate that drips from the moulds.

2. Measure out three-quarters of the tempered white chocolate and stir in the red food colouring with a rubber spatula until the colour is uniform. Fill the large egg moulds with the red-coloured chocolate and let them sit for 30 seconds. Invert the moulds on the wire rack and let the excess chocolate drain out. The shell should be $\frac{1}{16}$ inch (2 mm) thick. Refrigerate to set. As the chocolate sets in each mould, use a palette knife to scrape away any excess chocolate while keeping the mould inverted. The mould should be left with a very thin coat of red chocolate.

3. Set the remaining white chocolate aside to be retempered later.

4. Fill the cone moulds all the way to the top with one-quarter of the uncoloured tempered white chocolate for the beaks. Refrigerate for 3 to 5 minutes to set.

MAKE DARK CHOCOLATE COMPONENTS

1. Draw a large, thick V-shape for the eyebrows on a piece of baking paper with a pencil. The outline should be about $3\frac{1}{2}$ inches (9 cm) high and 3 inches (8 cm) wide at the open top of the V. Cut out the shape and set aside.

2. Remove the egg moulds from the refrigerator.

3. Melt and temper the dark chocolate (see page 242). Pour the tempered dark chocolate into the egg moulds on top of the red chocolate. Let the tempered chocolate sit in the moulds for 30 seconds. Invert the moulds to let the excess chocolate drain out. The shell should now be $\frac{1}{4}$ inch (6 mm) thick. Place the moulds (still inverted) on the wire rack. When the chocolate starts to set, use the palette knife to scrape away any excess chocolate from the edge. If the shell is still a little thin after the dark chocolate sets, add a second coat. Refrigerate about 30 minutes to set.

4. Meanwhile, line a baking tray with an acetate sheet. Place two 3-inch (8 cm) round ring moulds on the baking tray. Pour enough of the remaining tempered dark chocolate (which has been collected on the baking tray underneath the wire rack) into the ring moulds to create a base about $\frac{1}{2}$ inch (1.25 cm) thick. Refrigerate the ring moulds to set.

5. To create the eyebrows, spread a $\frac{1}{4}$-inch-thick (6 mm) layer of tempered dark chocolate onto a sheet of acetate. Let the chocolate set until it is no longer tacky, 4 to 5 minutes. Place the cut-out baking paper V-shape on top of the setting chocolate. Using a precision knife, cut along the out-

line of the eyebrow. Transfer the chocolate eyebrow to the baking tray and refrigerate to set. Repeat for a second eyebrow.

6. Set the remaining dark chocolate aside to be retempered later.

ASSEMBLE

1. Unmould the eggs by tapping the corner of the moulds on the work surface. If the chocolate is tempered properly, it should pop up immediately.

2. Bring the saucepan of water back to a simmer over medium heat. Place an inverted baking tray over the saucepan to warm. Let the tray heat until it is very warm to the touch, but not too hot. Place both halves of an egg, seam side down, on the surface of the baking tray and move them around a bit to melt the edges slightly. Before you seal the chocolate egg, place truffles, bonbons or other treats inside the cavity. Press the halves of the egg together to seal. Hold for a few seconds, then set aside. Repeat with the second egg.*

3. Place the base of the egg (still in the ring mould) on the baking tray and move it around a bit to melt it slightly. You will create a flat bottom for the base, so it can stand and support the egg.

4. Let the base set in the refrigerator for a few minutes, leaning on its side.

5. Retemper the remaining dark chocolate if necessary, and, using a rubber spatula, scoop a small amount into a piping bag or baking paper cornet. Cut an opening about ⅜ inch (1 cm) wide straight across the tip of the bag.

6. Unmould a base from a ring mould. Pipe a dot of tempered dark chocolate the size of a 5-cent coin in the centre of the base. Remove an egg from the refrigerator. Place the egg in the centre of the base standing straight up. Repeat with the other egg and base. Let them set for at least 20 minutes at room temperature or set with the cold spray.±

7. Pour yellow sanding sugar onto a plate. Remove the cones of white chocolate from the refrigerator and unmould them. With a heat gun, gently warm the outside of the cones and immediately roll into the yellow sanding sugar. Pipe a small dot of tempered dark chocolate on the flat side of the beak. Place the beak on the centre of the egg and set the chocolate with the cold spray, or simply hold it for a few minutes and then refrigerate to help it further set.

8. Retemper the remaining white and dark chocolate and place into separate cornets.

9. To create the eyes, pipe a dot of tempered white chocolate a little bit bigger than the size of a 10-cent coin on a sheet of acetate. Immediately pipe a dot of tempered dark chocolate in the centre for the pupil. Repeat for the three remaining eyes. Let them set for a few minutes and place in the refrigerator

* For even redder eggs, fill an airbrush with melted red cocoa butter and lightly spray the outside of the eggs. Refrigerate the eggs again.

± While the cold spray is not necessary, it does speed up the angry egg's drying process. Simply spray the base and egg once adhered.

if necessary. Pipe a small dot of tempered dark chocolate in the centre behind each eye. Place the eyes just above the beak and set with the cold spray or hold with your finger for a few minutes.

10. Pipe a small dot of tempered dark chocolate in the centre of an eyebrow. Place just above the eyes and set with the cold spray, or hold with your finger for a few moments until set. Repeat with the other egg and eyebrow.

SERVING INSTRUCTIONS The tradition is to hide the egg at Easter. Just remember that the real fun after you find it is to break it open and eat it!

STORAGE INSTRUCTIONS Can be kept in a closed airtight container in a cool dry place, away from direct light, for up to 1 week.

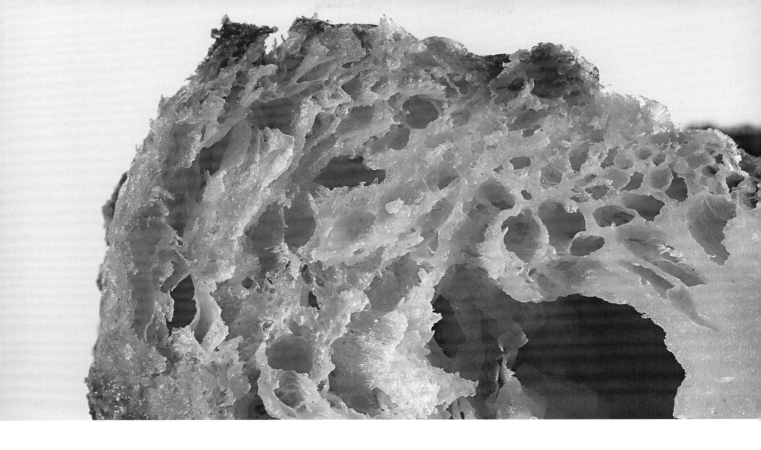

DOMINIQUE'S KOUIGN AMANNS (DKA)

I love making this recipe . . . because it can only be eaten fresh and will change your life when you do.

SKILL LEVEL Advanced
TIME 3 hours
YIELD 10 to 12 DKAs

INGREDIENTS

Strong flour	3 cups + 2 tablespoons	472 grams
Kosher salt	2 tablespoons	12 grams
Water, very cold	1¼ cups + 2½ tablespoons	313 grams
Unsalted butter *(84% butterfat)*, softened	26 tablespoons	364 grams
Instant yeast *(preferably SAF Gold Label)**	1½ teaspoons	4 grams
Cooking oil spray	as needed	as needed
Plain flour *(for dusting)*	as needed	as needed
Granulated sugar	about 1¾ cups	about 360 grams

SPECIAL TOOLS

Stand mixer with dough hook attachment
Ruler
Large offset spatula
Silicone baking mat
10 to 12 round ring moulds, 2¾ inch (7 cm) diameter
Stainless steel tongs

* Instant yeast is often used for doughs with higher sugar content, because this yeast needs less water to react and sugar tends to pull water from dough. You can substitute the same quantity of active dry yeast, but may get a denser final product.

MAKE DOUGH

1. Combine the strong flour, salt, water, 1 tablespoon (14 grams) of the butter and the yeast in a stand mixer fitted with a dough hook. Mix on low speed for 2 minutes to combine. Increase the speed to medium-high and beat for 10 minutes. When finished, the dough will be smooth and slightly tacky and will have full gluten development. Test by stretching it—the dough will have some elasticity.

2. Lightly grease a medium bowl with cooking oil spray. Transfer the dough to the bowl. Cover loosely with plastic wrap and proof at room temperature until doubled in size, about 1 hour.

3. Punch down the dough by folding the edges into the centre, releasing as much of the gas as possible, and turn it out onto a large sheet of plastic wrap. Using your palms, press it to form a 10-inch (25 cm) square. Wrap it tightly in the plastic wrap and place in the freezer for 15 minutes.

4. Flip the dough and return it to the freezer for another 15 minutes so that it chills evenly.

MAKE BUTTER BLOCK

1. While the dough is chilling, draw a 7-inch (18 cm) square on a piece of baking paper with a pencil. Flip the baking paper over so that the butter won't come in contact with the pencil marks. Place the remaining 25 tablespoons (350 grams) butter in the centre of the square and spread it evenly with an offset spatula to fill the square. Refrigerate the butter until firm but still pliable, about 20 minutes.*

2. Remove the butter from the refrigerator. It should still be soft enough to bend slightly without cracking. If it is too firm, lightly beat it with a rolling pin on a lightly floured work surface until it becomes pliable. Make sure to press the butter back to its original 7-inch (18 cm) square after working it.

3. Remove the dough from the freezer; make sure it is very cold throughout. Place the dough on a lightly floured work surface. Arrange the butter block in the centre of the dough so it looks like a diamond in the centre of the square (rotated 45 degrees, with the corners of the butter facing the centre of the dough sides). Pull the corners of the dough up and over to the centre of the butter block. Pinch the seams of the dough together to seal the butter inside. You should have a square slightly larger than the butter block.

4. With a rolling pin, using steady, even pressure, roll the dough out from the centre so that it triples in length. This will take several passes. Use extra flour to dust the work surface to ensure that nothing sticks. When finished, you should have a rectangle about 24 by 10 inches (60 by 25 cm) and ¼ inch (6 mm) thick.±

*   Whenever you are laminating dough, it is important that the consistency and temperature of the dough match those of the butter.

±   Keeping the dough's rectangular shape is very important at this point to ensure even layers throughout the process. You will need a large area to roll out the dough.

MAKE FIRST THREE FOLDS

1. Place the dough so the longer sides run left to right. From the right side fold one-third of the dough onto itself, keeping the edges lined up with each other. From the left side fold the remaining one-third of dough on top of the side that has already been folded. Line up all the edges so that you are left with an even rectangle. The dough is being folded as if it were a piece of paper going into an envelope; this is called a 'letter fold'. Do not rest the dough and immediately move on to the next fold.[‡]

2. Starting with the seam of the dough on the right, roll out the dough, vertically from top to bottom, to a rectangle about 24 by 10 inches (60 by 25 cm) and ¼ inch (6mm) thick. Repeat the letter fold.

3. Immediately roll out the dough again to a rectangle about 24 by 10 inches (60 by 25 cm) and ¼ inch (6 mm) thick exactly as in step 2. Repeat the letter fold. Wrap the dough in plastic wrap and refrigerate for 30 to 40 minutes to rest.

MAKE FOURTH FOLD

Sprinkle sugar in a thin, even layer on the work surface (as if you were flouring the work surface, but using sugar instead). Lay out the dough on the sugar. Starting with the seam of the dough on the right, roll out the dough once more, vertically from top to bottom, to a rectangle about 24 by 10 inches (60 by 25 cm) and ¼ inch (6 mm) thick. Sprinkle a thin, even layer of sugar on the top. Repeat the letter fold.[§]

ROLL, SHAPE, AND BAKE

1. Sprinkle another thin, even layer of sugar on the work surface. Place the dough on the sugar. Starting with the seam on the right, roll out the dough one final time to a rectangle about 24 by 10 inches (60 by 25 cm) and ¼ inch (6 mm) thick. Sprinkle another thin layer of sugar on top.

2. Using a chef's knife, cut the dough into 4-inch (10 cm) squares. Each square should weigh about 3½ ounces (100 grams). Sprinkle a little bit more sugar on the work surface. Fold in the corners of each square to meet at the centre, pushing the centre down firmly. Repeat with the new corners that were formed, again pushing down firmly in the centre.

3. Line a half baking tray with a silicone baking mat. Spray lightly with cooking oil spray and sprinkle with enough granulated sugar to just lightly coat it. Place the ring moulds 4 inches (10 cm) apart on the tray.

4. Place a square of dough in the centre of each ring. The dough will hang over the edges of the mould. Fold the excess dough into the centre of the DKA and press down firmly. Proof at room temperature, 15 to 20 minutes.

‡ When making the DKA, speed is very important. Work the dough as quickly as possible, otherwise it will soften and the butter will push out of the seams. This results in a dense and doughy product.

§ Work quickly when you add the sugar, as it will start to draw out moisture from the dough and make the surface wet.

5. While the DKAs are proofing, place a rack in the centre of the oven and preheat the oven to 365°F (185°C) for conventional or 340°F (170°C) for convection.

6. Bake the DKAs on the centre rack for 15 minutes. Rotate the tray 180 degrees and bake for 15 minutes more. The DKAs are finished when they turn golden brown and have about doubled in size.

7. Remove from the oven. Using a pair of stainless-steel tongs, unmould the DKAs onto a baking tray while still hot: Grab the metal rings with the tongs and flip the DKAs over so the flat side is up. Remove the rings. Let the DKAs cool completely, still inverted.

SERVING INSTRUCTIONS Enjoy at room temperature. If you are looking for more adventure, slice a DKA in half horizontally and add a scoop of ice cream to make an ice cream sandwich.

STORAGE INSTRUCTIONS DKAs should be consumed within 6 hours of baking.

MAGIC SOUFFLÉ

I love making this recipe . . . for the real pastry buffs who appreciate the delicate nature of its construction.

SKILL LEVEL Advanced

TIME 1 hour 30 minutes one day before; 1 hour the day of

YIELD 6 soufflés

INGREDIENTS

CHOCOLATE GANACHE

Pouring cream *(35% milk fat)*	⅓ cup + 3 tablespoons	100 grams
Dark chocolate *(70% cocoa content)*, finely chopped	½ cup	90 grams
Unsalted butter *(84% butterfat)*	2 tablespoons + 1 teaspoon	30 grams

ORANGE BLOSSOM BRIOCHE

Strong flour	2 cups	280 grams
Kosher salt	1 tablespoon	6 grams
Granulated sugar	¼ cup	51 grams
Instant yeast *(preferably SAF Gold Label)**	2 teaspoons	5 grams

TIMELINE

ONE DAY BEFORE Make ganache, dough and soufflé

THE DAY OF Assemble, proof and bake

SPECIAL TOOLS

Instant-read thermometer

Stand mixer with dough hook and whisk attachments

Siphon with carbon charger

6 rectangular ring moulds 2½ by 1¾ by 1¾ inches (6.5 by 4.5 by 4.5 cm)

---

*   Instant yeast is often used for doughs with higher sugar content, because this yeast needs less water to react and sugar tends to pull water from dough. You can substitute the same quantity of active dry yeast, but may get a denser final product.

Whole eggs (large)	4 each	4 each (200 grams)
Whole milk	1 tablespoon	15 grams
Unsalted butter *(84% butterfat)*, cold, cut in small dice	13 tablespoons	183 grams
Orange oil	½ teaspoon	1 gram
Grated orange zest	1 orange	1 orange
Orange blossom water	1 teaspoon	5 grams
Cooking oil spray	as needed	as needed
Plain flour (for dusting)	as needed	as needed
CHOCOLATE SOUFFLÉ		
Dark chocolate *(70% cocoa content)*, finely chopped	½ cup	98 grams
Unsalted butter *(84% butterfat)*	6½ tablespoons	91 grams
Granulated sugar	½ cup + 3 tablespoons	140 grams
Plain flour	¼ cup	30 grams
Baking powder	2½ tablespoons	10 grams
Whole eggs (large)	3 each	3 each (150 grams)

ONE DAY BEFORE

MAKE GANACHE

1. Bring the cream to a boil in a medium saucepan over medium heat. Remove from the heat.
2. Place the chocolate in a small heatproof bowl and pour the hot cream over it. Let stand for 30 seconds.
3. Whisk the chocolate and hot cream until smooth. Set aside to cool. When the ganache reaches 122°F (50°C), whisk in the butter until fully blended.*
4. Cover with plastic wrap pressed directly onto the surface of the ganache, to prevent a skin from forming. Refrigerate for 2 hours to set.

MAKE DOUGH±

1. Combine the strong flour, salt, sugar, yeast and eggs in a stand mixer fitted with a dough hook. Mix on low speed until the dough forms a ball. Slowly pour in the milk and mix on low until combined. Increase the speed to medium-high for 6 to 8 minutes more to develop the gluten, which will help the dough hold its structure. It should pull off the sides of the bowl cleanly when it's ready. Check the dough using the 'windowpane test' (see page 151).
2. When the dough has reached full gluten development, add the butter, keeping the mixer on medium-high speed. Mix just until the butter is incorporated. Add the orange oil, orange zest and orange blossom water and mix until fully incorporated. The finished dough should be smooth, shiny and sticky.

* If you add the butter while the ganache is still hot, the butter will melt and the ganache will have a grainy consistency when it sets.

± This recipe yields more brioche than needed. Bake the extra dough and enjoy a brioche roll for breakfast.

3. Lightly grease a medium bowl with cooking oil spray. Transfer the dough to the bowl. Cover with plastic wrap pressed directly onto the surface of the dough, to prevent a skin from forming. Proof the dough at room temperature (no warmer than 75°F/24°C) until doubled in size, about 1 hour 30 minutes.

4. Remove the plastic wrap and punch down the dough by folding the edges into the centre, releasing as much of the gas as possible. Cover the dough again with plastic wrap pressed directly on the surface. Refrigerate overnight to relax the gluten.

MAKE SOUFFLÉ

1. Melt the chocolate and butter in a small bowl on high power in 20-second intervals in the microwave, stirring with a heatproof spatula between intervals, until smooth.

2. Combine the granulated sugar, plain flour, baking powder and eggs in a stand mixer fitted with a whisk. Mix on low speed for a few minutes until just incorporated.

3. With the mixer on low speed, stream in the melted chocolate and butter. With a rubber spatula, scrape down the sides of the bowl. Whip on high speed for 3 minutes, until the batter is smooth. Cover with plastic wrap pressed directly against the surface of the batter and refrigerate for 1 hour.

4. While the soufflé batter is chilling, place a rack in the centre of the oven and preheat the oven to 375°F (190°C) for conventional or 350°F (175°C) for convection.

5. Using a rubber spatula, place 2 large scoops of soufflé batter in a siphon, so that it is half full.

6. Line a baking tray with baking paper and arrange the rectangular ring moulds about 2 inches (5 cm) apart. Grease the insides of the moulds with cooking oil spray. Pipe soufflé batter into the moulds until they are about halfway full. Add a dollop of chocolate ganache with a spoon to the centre of each mould. Cover with soufflé batter to fill. Bake for 4 minutes. Rotate the tray 180 degrees and bake for 4 minutes more.

7. When fully baked, place the soufflés, still in the moulds, in the freezer to set overnight.

THE DAY OF
ASSEMBLE AND PROOF

1. Pull one-third of the dough from the refrigerator. On a lightly floured surface, use a rolling pin to roll out the dough into a rectangle measuring 20 by 10 inches (50 by 25 cm). Place on a baking tray lined with baking paper and refrigerate. Let the dough rest in the refrigerator for 30 minutes to relax the gluten.

2. Using a chef's knife, cut the brioche dough into 6 by 3–inch (15 by 8 cm) strips. Return the cut dough to the refrigerator until needed.

3. Run a thin-bladed knife around the inside of the ring moulds and lift off the mould to unmould the chocolate soufflés. Place a soufflé in the centre of a rectangle of brioche and wrap the brioche around the soufflé as tightly as possible. Fold and pinch the ends of the brioche together to cover the top and bottom of the soufflé. Cut off any excess dough with a paring knife. Repeat until all the remaining soufflés are wrapped.[‡]

4. Wash and dry the ring moulds. Lightly grease the inside of the moulds with cooking oil spray. Place each wrapped soufflé inside of a mould (it will be a very tight fit). Transfer the moulds to a baking tray lined with baking paper.

5. Lightly lay a piece of plastic wrap over the magic soufflés. Proof them at room temperature until they reach the top of the mould, about 2 hours.

6. Return the magic soufflés to the freezer to chill for 1 hour.

BAKE

1. Place a rack in the centre of the oven and preheat the oven to 400°F (205°C) for conventional or 375°F (190°C) for convection.

2. Remove the plastic wrap and lay a piece of baking paper on top of the soufflés, followed by a second baking tray. This helps compress them while they bake. If you do not have a second baking tray, substitute something of equal weight—just make sure the object has a flat bottom.

3. Bake the soufflés on the centre rack for 5 minutes. Rotate the tray 180 degrees and bake for 5 minutes more or until they are golden brown.[§] Remove from the oven and unmould immediately. They are unlikely to stick.

4. Let cool for 5 minutes before serving.

[‡] When covering the soufflé with the brioche dough, just think of it as a present you're wrapping. You don't want people to see what is inside, so make sure the soufflé is completely covered.

[§] If you're using a conventional oven, you will have to turn the soufflés over after the first 5 minutes so that the bottom is facing up. With conventional ovens the heat comes only from the bottom, which means the bottom will bake much more quickly than the top.

SERVING INSTRUCTIONS Serve within 15 minutes of baking to ensure the centre is still molten.

STORAGE INSTRUCTIONS This does not store well, unfortunately, as the molten centre will dry out over time. The leftover dough can be baked for breakfast.

THE AT-HOME CRONUT™ PASTRY

I love making this recipe . . . because—what can I say?—it changed the world. This is a version designed for the home cook.

SKILL LEVEL Advanced

TIME 1 hour two days before; 1 hour one day before; 2 hours the day of

YIELD 12 At-Home Cronut™ pastries

INGREDIENTS

Ganache of your choice (pages 205 to 207)	1 batch	1 batch
Flavoured sugar of your choice (page 208)		
Glaze of your choice (page 208)		

AT-HOME CRONUT™ PASTRY DOUGH

Strong flour	3¾ cups, plus more as needed for dusting	525 grams, plus more as needed for dusting
Kosher salt	1 tablespoon + 2 teaspoons	6 grams
Granulated sugar	¼ cup + 1 tablespoon	64 grams

TIMELINE

TWO DAYS BEFORE Make ganache, At-Home Cronut™ pastry dough and butter block

ONE DAY BEFORE Laminate

THE DAY OF Cut and fry dough; make glaze and flavoured sugar; assemble

SPECIAL TOOLS

Stand mixer with dough hook and whisk attachments

Ruler

Large offset spatula

3½-inch (9 cm) ring cutter

1 inch (2.5 cm) ring cutter

Deep-frying thermometer

2 uncut piping bags

Ingredient	Volume	Weight	Equipment
Instant yeast (preferably SAF Gold Label)*	1 tablespoon + 1½ teaspoons	11 grams	Wilton #230 Bismarck metal tip or other Bismarck tube
Water, cold	1 cup + 2 tablespoons	250 grams	Ateco #803 plain tip (5⁄16-inch/ 0.8 cm diameter)
Egg white (large)	1 each	1 each (30 grams)	
Unsalted butter (84% butterfat), softened	8 tablespoons	112 grams	
Pouring cream (35% milk fat)	1 tablespoon	15 grams	
Cooking oil spray	as needed	as needed	
BUTTER BLOCK			
Unsalted butter (84% butterfat), softened	18 tablespoons	251 grams	
Grapeseed oil	as needed	as needed	
Glaze of your choice (page 208)	as needed	as needed	
Decorating sugar of your choice (page 208)	as needed	as needed	

* Instant yeast is often used for doughs with higher sugar content, because this yeast needs less water to react and sugar tends to pull water from dough. You can substitute the same quantity of active dry yeast, but may get a denser final product.

TWO DAYS BEFORE

MAKE GANACHE

Prepare one of the ganache recipes on pages 205 to 207 and refrigerate until needed.

MAKE AT-HOME CRONUT™ PASTRY DOUGH

1. Combine the strong flour, salt, sugar, yeast, water, egg whites, butter and cream in a stand mixer fitted with a dough hook. Mix until just combined, about 3 minutes. When finished the dough will be rough and have very little gluten development.

2. Lightly grease a medium bowl with cooking oil spray. Transfer the dough to the bowl. Cover with plastic wrap pressed directly on the surface of the dough, to prevent a skin from forming. Proof the dough in a warm spot until doubled in size, 2 to 3 hours.

3. Remove the plastic wrap and punch down the dough by folding the edges into the centre, releasing as much of the gas as possible. On a piece of baking paper, shape into a 10-inch (25 cm) square. Transfer to a baking tray, still on the baking paper, and cover with plastic wrap. Refrigerate overnight.

MAKE BUTTER BLOCK

Draw a 7-inch (18 cm) square on a piece of baking paper with a pencil. Flip the paper over so that the butter won't come in contact with the pencil marks. Place the butter in the centre of the square and spread it evenly with an offset spatula to fill the square. Refrigerate overnight.

ONE DAY BEFORE

LAMINATE

1. Remove the butter from the refrigerator. It should still be soft enough to

bend slightly without cracking. If it is still too firm, lightly beat it with a rolling pin on a lightly floured work surface until it becomes pliable. Make sure to press the butter back to its original 7-inch (18 cm) square after working it.

2. Remove the dough from the refrigerator, making sure it is very cold throughout. Place the dough on a floured work surface. Using the rolling pin, roll out the dough to a 10-inch (25.5 cm) square about 1 inch (2.5 cm) thick. Arrange the butter block in the centre of the dough so it looks like a diamond in the centre of the square (rotated 45 degrees, with the corners of the butter block facing the centre of the dough sides). Pull the corners of the dough up and over to the centre of the butter block. Pinch the seams of dough together to seal the butter inside. You should have a square slightly larger than the butter block.

3. Very lightly dust the work surface with flour to ensure the dough doesn't stick. With a rolling pin, using steady, even pressure, roll out the dough from the centre. When finished, you should have a 20-inch (50 cm) square about ¼ inch (6 mm) thick.*

4. Fold the dough in half horizontally, making sure to line up the edges so you are left with a rectangle. Then fold the dough vertically. You should have a 10-inch (25.5 cm) square of dough with 4 layers. Wrap tightly in plastic wrap and refrigerate for 1 hour.

5. Repeat steps 3 and 4. Cover tightly with plastic wrap and refrigerate overnight.

THE DAY OF

CUT DOUGH

1. On a lightly floured work surface, roll out the dough to a 15-inch (40 cm) square about ½ inch (1.3 cm) thick. Transfer the dough to a half baking tray, cover with plastic wrap, and refrigerate for 1 hour to relax.

2. Using a 3½-inch (9 cm) ring cutter, cut 12 rounds. Cut out the centre of each round with a 1-inch (2.5 cm) ring cutter to create the doughnut shape.

3. Line a baking tray with baling paper and lightly dust the paper with flour. Place the At-Home Cronut™ pastries on the tray, spacing them about 3 inches (8 cm) apart. Lightly spray a piece of plastic wrap with cooking oil spray and lay it on top of the pastries. Proof in a warm spot until tripled in size, about 2 hours.±

FRY DOUGH

1. Heat the grapeseed oil in a large saucepan until it reaches 350°F (175°C). Use a deep-frying thermometer to verify the oil is at the right temperature.‡ Line a platter with several layers of paper towels for draining.

2. Gently place 3 or 4 of them at a time into the hot oil. Fry for about 90 seconds on each side, flipping once, until golden brown. Remove from the oil with a slotted spoon and drain on the paper towels.

* This is not the typical lamination technique and is unique to this recipe.
  When rolling out dough, you want to use as little flour as possible. The more flour you incorporate into the dough, the tougher it will be to roll out, and when you fry the At-Home Cronut™ pastries they will flake apart.

± It's best to proof At-Home Cronut pastries in a warm, humid place. But if the proofing area is too warm, the butter will melt, so do not place the pastries on top of the oven or near another direct source of heat.

‡ The temperature of the oil is very important to the frying process. If it is too low, the pastries will be greasy; too high, the inside will be undercooked while the outside is burnt.

3. Check that the oil is at the right temperature. If not, let it heat up again before frying the next batch. Continue until all of them are fried.

4. Let cool completely before filling.

MAKE GLAZE

Prepare the glaze on page 208 that corresponds to your choice of ganache.

MAKE FLAVOURED SUGAR

Prepare the decorating sugar on page 208 that corresponds to your choice of ganache.

ASSEMBLE

1. Transfer the ganache to a stand mixer fitted with a whisk. Whip on high speed until the ganache holds a stiff peak. (If using the Champagne-chocolate ganache, simply whisk it until smooth. It will be quite thick already.)

2. Cut the tip of a piping bag to snugly fit the Bismarck tip. Using a rubber spatula, place 2 large scoops of ganache in a piping bag so that it is one-third full. Push the ganache down toward the tip of the bag.

3. Place the decorating sugar that corresponds to your choice of ganache and glaze in a bowl.

4. Arrange each At-Home Cronut™ pastry so that the flatter side is facing up. Inject the ganache through the top of the pastry in four different spots, evenly spaced. As you pipe the ganache, you should feel the pastry getting heavier in your hand.

5. Place the pastry on its side. Roll in the corresponding sugar, coating the outside edges.

6. If the glaze has cooled, microwave it for a few seconds to warm until soft. Cut the tip of a piping bag to snugly fit a #803 plain tip. Using a rubber spatula, transfer the glaze to the bag. Push the glaze down toward the tip of the bag.

7. Pipe a ring of glaze around the top of each At-Home Cronut pastry, making sure to cover all the holes created from the filling. Keep in mind that the glaze will continue to spread slightly as it cools. Let the glaze set for about 15 minutes before serving.

....

SERVING INSTRUCTIONS Because the At-Home Cronut™ pastry is cream-filled, it must be served at room temperature.

STORAGE INSTRUCTIONS Consume within 8 hours of frying. Leftover ganache can be stored in a closed airtight container in the refrigerator for 2 days. Leftover flavoured sugar can keep in a closed airtight container for weeks and can be used to macerate fruits or sweeten drinks.

GANACHES

VANILLA ROSE GANACHE

YIELD Ganache for 12 At-Home Cronut™ pastries

INGREDIENTS

Gelatine sheet (160 bloom)*	1 each	1 each
Pouring cream *(35% milk fat)*	1¾ cups	406 grams
Vanilla bean *(preferably Tahitian),* split lengthwise, seeds scraped	1 each	1 each
White chocolate, finely chopped	½ cup	90 grams
Rose water	4 tablespoons	50 grams

* If you can't find gelatine sheets, use powdered gelatine.
  One gelatine sheet = 1 scant teaspoon (2.3 grams) powdered gelatine.
  For every teaspoon of gelatine, bloom in 1 tablespoon (15 grams) water.

1. Soak the gelatine sheet in a bowl of ice water until soft, about 20 minutes. If using powdered gelatine, sprinkle 1 teaspoon (2.3 grams) gelatine over 1 tablespoon (15 grams) water in a small bowl, stir, and let sit 20 minutes to bloom.

2. Combine the pouring cream and vanilla bean seeds in a small saucepan and bring to a boil over medium heat. Remove from the heat.

3. If using a gelatine sheet, squeeze out any excess water. Whisk the bloomed gelatine into the cream until the gelatine is dissolved.

4. Place the white chocolate in a small heatproof bowl. Pour the hot cream over the chocolate and let stand for 30 seconds.

5. Whisk the white chocolate and hot cream until smooth. Add the rose water and whisk until fully blended. Cover with plastic wrap pressed directly onto the surface of the ganache, to prevent a skin from forming. Refrigerate overnight to set.

WHIPPED LEMON GANACHE

YIELD Ganache for 12 At-Home Cronut™ pastries

INGREDIENTS

Gelatine sheet (160 bloom)*	2 each	2 each
Pouring cream *(35% milk fat)*	¾ cup + 2 tablespoons	188 grams
Grated lemon zest	1 lemon	1 lemon
Granulated sugar	¼ cup	51 grams
White chocolate, finely chopped	¾ cup	117 grams
Lemon juice	½ cup + 1 tablespoon	141 grams

* If you can't find gelatine sheets, use powdered gelatine.
  One gelatine sheet = 1 scant teaspoon (2.3 grams) powdered gelatine.
  For every teaspoon of gelatine, bloom in 1 tablespoon (15 grams) water.

1. Soak the gelatine sheets in a bowl of ice water until soft, about 20 minutes. If using powdered gelatine, sprinkle 2 teaspoons (5 grams) gelatine over 2 tablespoons (30 grams) water in a small bowl, stir, and let sit 20 minutes to bloom.

2. Combine the cream, lemon zest, and sugar in a small saucepan and bring to a boil over medium heat. Remove from the heat.

3. If using gelatine sheets, squeeze out any excess water. Whisk the bloomed gelatine into the cream until the gelatine is dissolved.

4. Place the white chocolate in a small heatproof bowl. Pour the hot cream over the chocolate and let stand for 30 seconds.

5. Whisk the white chocolate and hot cream until smooth. Let the ganache cool to room temperature.

6. Whisk in the lemon juice. Cover with plastic wrap pressed directly onto the surface of the ganache, to prevent a skin from forming. Refrigerate overnight to set.

CHAMPAGNE-CHOCOLATE GANACHE

YIELD Ganache for 12 At-Home Cronut™ pastries

INGREDIENTS

Water	2 tablespoons	26 grams
Champagne	¼ cup + 2 tablespoons	102 grams
Unsweetened cocoa powder	1½ tablespoons	9 grams
Pouring cream (*35% milk fat*)	½ cup	115 grams
Egg yolks (large)	3 each	3 each (60 grams)
Granulated sugar	3 tablespoons	38 grams
Dark chocolate (*66% cocoa content*), finely chopped	1 cup + 1 tablespoon	165 grams

1. Combine the water, 2 tablespoons (26 grams) of the Champagne and the cocoa powder in a small bowl. Mix to a smooth paste.
2. Combine the cream and the remaining ¼ cup (76 grams) Champagne in a small saucepan and bring to a boil over medium heat. Remove from the heat.
3. Whisk the egg yolks and granulated sugar together in a small bowl. Stream one-third of the hot cream mixture into the egg yolks, whisking constantly until fully blended, to temper them. Whisk the tempered yolks into the remaining hot cream. Return the saucepan to medium heat.
4. Keep whisking! Continue to cook the custard over medium heat until it reaches 185°F (85°C). The custard will turn pale yellow and thicken so that it coats the back of a spoon. Remove from the heat and whisk in the cocoa powder paste until fully incorporated.
5. Place the chocolate in a medium heatproof bowl. Strain the custard through a small sieve over the chocolate. Let stand for 30 seconds.
6. Whisk the chocolate and custard until smooth. When finished, the ganache will have the consistency of yoghurt. Reserve ¼ cup (50 grams) for the glaze. Cover with plastic wrap pressed directly onto the surface of the ganache, to prevent a skin from forming. Refrigerate overnight to set.

FLAVOURED SUGARS

YIELD About 1 cup (200 grams) each

INGREDIENTS

VANILLA SUGAR

Granulated sugar	1 cup	205 grams
Vanilla bean *(preferably Tahitian),* split lengthwise, seeds scraped	1 each	1 each

MAPLE SUGAR

Granulated maple sugar	1 cup	200 grams
Grated lemon zest	1 lemon	1 lemon

ORANGE SUGAR

Granulated sugar	1 cup	205 grams
Grated orange zest	1 orange	1 orange

Combine the sugar and its flavouring in a small bowl. Reserve until needed.

GLAZES

YIELD About ½ cup (200 grams) each

INGREDIENTS

ROSE GLAZE

Glazing fondant*	½ cup	200 grams
Rose water	2 tablespoons	30 grams

LEMON GLAZE

Glazing fondant*	½ cup	200 grams
Grated lemon zest	1 lemon	1 lemon

CHAMPAGNE-CHOCOLATE GLAZE

Glazing fondant*	½ cup	200 grams
Champagne-chocolate ganache (page 207)	¼ cup	50 grams

* Glazing fondant is also known as 'fondant icing' or 'pastry fondant'. It is similar to royal icing but remains shiny when it sets.

Warm the fondant in a small bowl in the microwave in 10-second intervals, stirring between intervals. When the fondant is slightly warm, about 20 seconds, add the corresponding flavour and stir until fully blended.

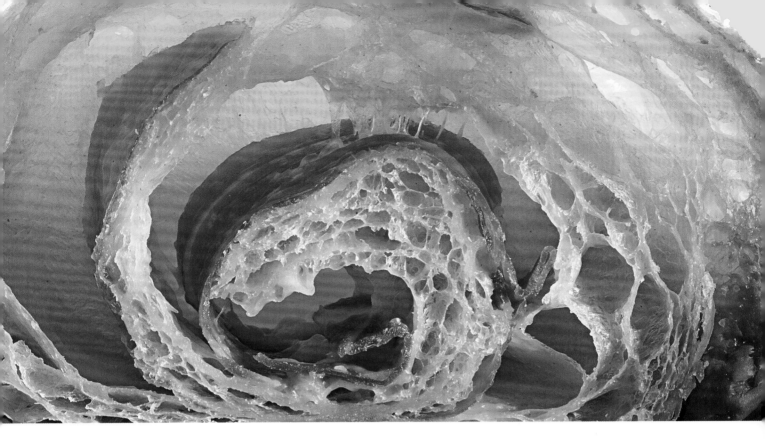

IBÉRICO AND MAHÓN CROISSANT

I love making this recipe . . . as the perfect brunch item and an amazing afternoon snack.

SKILL LEVEL Advanced

TIME 1 hour 30 minutes two days before; 2 hours one day before; 1 hour the day of

YIELD 12 to 15 croissants

INGREDIENTS

CROISSANT DOUGH

Strong flour	3¾ cups, plus more as needed for dusting	525 grams, plus more as needed for dusting
Kosher salt	1 tablespoon + 1 teaspoon	10 grams
Granulated sugar	⅓ cup + 1 tablespoon	80 grams
Instant yeast *(preferably SAF Gold Label)**	1 tablespoon + 2 teaspoons	13 grams
Water	1 cup	250 grams
Unsalted butter *(84% butterfat)*, softened	8 tablespoons	112 grams

* Instant yeast is often used for doughs with higher sugar content, because this yeast needs less water to react and sugar tends to pull water from dough. You can substitute the same quantity of active dry yeast, but you may get a denser final product.

TIMELINE

TWO DAYS BEFORE Make dough; prepare pork fat and dried ham; make butter block

ONE DAY BEFORE Make three folds; roll, fill and shape

THE DAY OF Bake

SPECIAL TOOLS

Stand mixer with dough hook attachment (and paddle attachment, optional)

Ruler

Large offset spatula

Pastry brush

Cooking oil spray	as needed	as needed
Ibérico ham, very thinly sliced	24 to 30 slices	24 to 30 slices

BUTTER BLOCK

Unsalted butter *(84% butterfat)*, softened	16 tablespoons	224 grams
Rendered pork fat (step 1, below)	1 tablespoon	13 grams
Mahón cheese, sliced	12 to 15 slices	12 to 15 slices
Mahón cheese, grated	⅓ cup, loosely packed	30 grams
Egg wash *(2 eggs, 1 pinch salt and a dash of milk, beaten together)*	as needed	as needed

....

TWO DAYS BEFORE

MAKE DOUGH

1. Combine the strong flour, salt, sugar, yeast, water and butter in a stand mixer fitted with a dough hook. Mix on low speed about 3 minutes, until just combined. When finished, the dough will be rough and have very little gluten development.

2. Lightly grease a medium bowl with cooking oil spray. Transfer the dough into the bowl and cover with plastic wrap pressed directly on the dough, to prevent a skin from forming. Proof the dough in a warm spot until doubled in size, 1 hour 30 minutes to 2 hours.

3. Remove the plastic wrap and punch down the dough by folding the edges into the centre, releasing as much of the gas as possible. On a piece of baking paper, shape the dough into a 10-inch (25 cm) square. Place the dough, still on the baking paper, on a baking tray and cover with plastic wrap. Refrigerate overnight.

PREPARE PORK FAT AND DRIED HAM

1. Trim the fat from the edges of all slices of Ibérico ham. Cook the trimmings in a small saucepan over low heat until the fat has liquefied. Strain through a small sieve into a small bowl. Discard any solids left in the sieve. Cover the bowl of fat with plastic wrap and refrigerate for about 30 minutes, until solid.

2. While the fat is chilling, place a rack in the centre of the oven and preheat the oven to 350°F (175°C) for conventional or 325°F (160°C) for convection. Line a baking tray with baking paper. Line a platter with paper towels.

3. Set 15 pieces of ham aside. These will be used to roll inside the croissants. Lay out the remaining slices of ham on the lined tray. Bake

on the centre rack for about 10 minutes. Rotate the tray 180 degrees and bake for 10 minutes more or until the slices are crispy throughout. Drain and cool the ham slices on the paper towels. When completely cooled, chop into small bits. You should have about 1 tablespoon (60 grams), loosely packed.

MAKE BUTTER BLOCK

1. Combine the butter, the rendered fat and chopped ham in a stand mixer fitted with a paddle and mix on low speed until blended. Try not to incorporate too much air.

2. Draw a 7-inch (18 cm) square on a piece of baking paper with a pencil. Flip the paper over so that the butter mixture won't come in contact with the pencil marks. Place the butter in the centre of the square and spread it evenly with an offset spatula to fill the square. Refrigerate overnight.

ONE DAY BEFORE
MAKE THREE FOLDS

1. Remove the butter mixture from the refrigerator. It should still be soft enough to bend slightly without cracking. If it is too firm, lightly beat it with a rolling pin on a lightly floured work surface until it becomes pliable. Make sure to press the butter back to its 7-inch (18 cm) square after working it.

2. Remove the dough from the refrigerator, making sure it is very cold throughout. Place the dough on a lightly floured work surface. Arrange the butter block in the centre of the dough so it looks like a diamond in the centre of the square (rotated 45 degrees, with the corners of the butter block facing the centre of the dough sides). Pull the corners of the dough up and over to the centre of the butter block. Pinch the seams of dough together to seal the butter inside. You should have a square slightly larger than the butter block.

3. Lightly dust the work surface with flour to ensure that the dough won't stick. With a rolling pin, using steady, even pressure, roll out the dough from the centre so that it triples in length. This will take several passes. When finished, you should have a rectangle about 24 by 10 inches (60 by 25 cm) and ¼ inch (6 mm) thick.

4. Place the dough so the longer sides run left to right. From the right side, fold one-third of the dough onto itself, keeping the edges lined up with each other. From the left side, fold the remaining one-third of dough on top of the side that has already been folded. Line up all the edges so that you are left with a square. The dough is being folded as if it were a piece of paper going into an envelope, so this is called a 'letter

fold'. Wrap the dough tightly in plastic wrap and refrigerate for about 1 hour to relax the gluten.

5. Repeat steps 3 and 4 for your second fold.

6. With the seam always on the right, roll out the dough vertically from top to bottom, rotate the dough 90 degrees, and repeat the letter fold once more. Do this again, making a third letter fold, with the seams to the right. Refrigerate the dough for 1 hour between folds. Wrap the dough tightly in plastic wrap and refrigerate for 1 hour.

7. Place the dough on a lightly floured work surface. With a rolling pin, using steady, even pressure, roll out the dough from the centre vertically from top to bottom so that it triples in length. This will take several passes. When finished, you should have a rectangle about 24 by 10 inches (60 by 25 cm) and ¼ inch (6 mm) thick. Cover it lightly with plastic wrap and refrigerate for 1 hour to rest.*

8. Lightly flour the work surface and lay the dough flat. Using a ruler, starting from the left side, score the dough every 3 inches (8 cm) along the bottom edge until you reach the right side of the dough. Make the first score on the top edge 1½ inches (4 cm) from the left end. Continue scoring the top edge every 3 inches (8 cm). These staggered marks should give a nice guideline for cutting triangles. Use a large chef's knife to connect each score mark on the top with the two at bottom on either side of it. The isosceles triangles should measure 3 inches (8 cm) wide and 10 inches (25 cm) high. There will be narrow triangles of dough left over at each end.

9. Gently stretch the cut triangles an additional 2 to 3 inches (5 to 8 cm) in length, being careful not to tear the dough.‡

ROLL, FILL, AND SHAPE

1. Lay 1 slice of the reserved Ibérico ham on each triangle of croissant dough, keeping the ham inside the borders of the dough. At the wide end of each dough triangle, place a slice of Mahón cheese.‡

2. Starting at the wide end, roll the croissant dough toward the tip, keeping steady, even pressure as you roll. When finished, make sure the tip of the dough is on the bottom of the croissant.

3. Line a baking tray with baking paper. Place the croissants on the baking tray about 4 inches (10 cm) apart. Lightly lay a piece of plastic wrap over the croissants and refrigerate overnight.

THE DAY OF

BAKE

1. Remove the tray of croissants from the refrigerator. Keep them lightly covered in plastic wrap. Proof at room temperature until tripled in size, 1 hour 30 minutes to 2 hours.

* If you don't have enough space in the refrigerator, you can gently fold the dough in half to fit.

± Stretching out the dough not only gives you more to roll, it also relaxes the dough.

‡ The Mahón cheese will need to be broken up to fit into the triangle.

2. Place a rack in the centre of the oven and preheat the oven to 375°F (190°C) for conventional or 350°F (175°C) for convection.

3. Lightly brush the croissants with egg wash and sprinkle with grated Mahón cheese, about 1 teaspoon per croissant. Bake on the centre rack for 8 minutes. Rotate the tray 180 degrees and bake for 8 minutes more or until golden brown. Remove from the oven and let cool briefly.

SERVING INSTRUCTIONS Best served fresh and hot out of the oven.

STORAGE INSTRUCTIONS Croissants should be eaten within 5 hours of baking.

SWEET POTATO MONT BLANC

I love making this recipe . . . because it is a mix of textures: creamy, crispy, chewy and crumbly.

SKILL LEVEL Advanced

TIME 5 hours one day before; 45 minutes the day of

YIELD 6 individual Mont Blancs

INGREDIENTS

Swiss meringue (page 116)	1 batch	1 batch
Sablé Breton cookie dough (page 126), unbaked	1 batch	1 batch

CITRUS MARMALADE

Orange	1 orange	1 orange
Lemons	1½ lemons	1½ lemons
Granulated sugar	⅓ cup	68 grams
Grapefruit juice	2 tablespoons	31 grams
Orange juice	2 tablespoons	31 grams
Lime juice	2 tablespoons	31 grams
Lemon juice	2 tablespoons	31 grams
Finely chopped lemon zest	1 lemon	1 lemon

TIMELINE

ONE DAY BEFORE Make meringues, sablé cookie dough, marmalade, purée, mousse and Chantilly cream; begin assembly

THE DAY OF Bake sablé cookies; finish assembly

SPECIAL TOOLS

3 uncut piping bags

Ateco #804 plain tip (⅜-inch/ 1 cm diameter)

6 silicone cone moulds*

* The mould I recommend is silicone, about 3 inches (7.5 cm) high, cone-shaped, with a flat top about 1 inch (2.5 cm) across the point and a 1½-inch (3.75 cm) square base. If you don't have this mould, simply adjust the size of the sablé cookie to match the base of the mould you have.

SWEET POTATO PURÉE

Granulated sugar	2¼ cups	461 grams
Water	2 cups + 4 tablespoons	500 grams
Sweet potatoes, small, whole, skin on	10½ ounces	300 grams

SWEET POTATO MOUSSE

Gelatine sheet (160 bloom)*	1 each	1 each
Pouring cream *(35% milk fat)*	½ cup + 1 tablespoon	118 grams
Dark rum	1 tablespoon	15 grams
Light brown sugar	2 tablespoons + 2 teaspoons	30 grams
Unsalted butter *(84% butterfat)*	1½ tablespoons	21 grams
Sweet potato purée (from above)	¾ cup	189 grams
Vanilla Chantilly Cream (page 185), unwhipped	2 batches	2 batches
Icing sugar *(for serving, optional)*	as needed	as needed

Blender or food processor

Small offset spatula

Stand mixer with whisk
attachment

1½-inch (3.75 cm) ring cutter,
or one that fits the bottom of
the mould

Sieve (optional)

----

* If you can't find gelatine sheets, use powdered gelatine.
  One gelatine sheet = 1 scant teaspoon (2.3 grams) powdered gelatine.
  For every teaspoon of gelatine, bloom in 1 tablespoon (15 grams) water.

ONE DAY BEFORE

MAKE MERINGUES

1. Make Swiss meringue, page 116. Preheat the oven to 200°F (95°C) for conventional or 175°F (80°C) for convection.

2. Cut the tip of a piping bag to snugly fit a #804 plain tip. Using a rubber spatula, place 2 large scoops of Swiss meringue in the bag so that it is one-third full. Push the meringue down toward the tip of the bag.

3. Line a baking tray with baking paper. At each corner, pipe a small dot of meringue under the baking paper and push the paper flat. This will help keep it 'glued' to the baking tray. Holding the piping bag at a 90 degree angle about ½ inch (1.25 cm) above the pan, pipe the meringue with steady, even pressure. Pipe at least 6 small teardrops, just over 1 inch (3 cm) wide and just over 1 inch (3 cm) tall.*

4. Wet your finger slightly and press down on the peaks of the teardrops to flatten them. The meringues should be shaped like thick buttons.±

5. Bake for 20 minutes. Rotate the tray 180 degrees and bake for 20 minutes more. Continue to rotate every 20 minutes until the meringues are completely dry, about 1 hour 20 minutes.

6. Let the meringues, still on the baking paper, cool completely. The meringues should be crispy all the way through, with no moisture on the inside. Reserve in an airtight container in a cool, dry space.

* It is always good to pipe a few extra meringues just to be safe. They tend to break easily.

± If you have leftover meringue, try making Mini Me's (page 116).

MAKE SABLÉ COOKIE DOUGH

Make sablé cookie dough, page 126. Roll out the sablé cookie dough to a rectangle a little larger than 6 by 9 inches (15 by 23 cm). Wrap tightly between two sheets of baking paper and let it rest overnight in the refrigerator.

MAKE MARMALADE

1. While the meringues are baking, cut the top and bottom off the orange and the lemon. Trim as much of the peel and pith off the fruit as possible without cutting into the segments of citrus. Cut the peel into extremely thin strips, about the thickness of a credit card.
2. Combine the lemon and orange peels in a small saucepan. Fill the saucepan with enough cold water to completely cover the peels. Place on high heat and bring to a boil. Remove from the heat and drain. Repeat this process 2 more times. This blanching process helps you eliminate the bitterness from the peels.
3. Drain the blanched orange and lemon peels, return them to the saucepan, and add the sugar and the grapefruit, orange, lime and lemon juices. Bring to a boil over high heat and then lower the heat to a simmer. Simmer for about 30 minutes, stirring occasionally to make sure the marmalade doesn't burn. As it cooks, it will thicken and the orange and lemon peels will become tender.
4. Add the finely chopped lemon zest.
5. Transfer the marmalade to a small bowl and let cool to room temperature. When fully cooled, cover with plastic wrap and refrigerate.

MAKE PURÉE

1. Combine the granulated sugar and water in a medium saucepan and bring to a boil. Add the sweet potatoes. Reduce the heat to a simmer and cook until the sweet potatoes are tender, about 30 minutes. You should be able to slide a knife through them with no resistance. Drain the sweet potatoes (discard the syrup) and let them cool for 15 to 20 minutes.
2. While the sweet potatoes are still warm, peel off the skin with a paring knife.‡
3. Purée the sweet potatoes in a blender or food processor until smooth. Measure out ¾ cup (189 grams) into a medium bowl, cover with plastic wrap, and reserve at room temperature.

‡ Peeling the sweet potatoes while they are still warm ensures the skin will come off much more easily.

MAKE MOUSSE

1. Soak the gelatine sheet in a bowl of ice water until soft, about 20 minutes. If using powdered gelatine, sprinkle 1 teaspoon (2.3 grams) gelatine over 1 tablespoon (15 grams) water in a small bowl, stir, and let sit 20 minutes to bloom.

2. Whip the pouring cream with a whisk to medium peaks in a medium bowl. The cream should fall back onto itself. Cover with plastic wrap and refrigerate until needed.

3. Combine the rum and brown sugar in a small saucepan. Bring to a boil over high heat to dissolve the sugar. Remove from the heat.

4. If using a gelatine sheet, squeeze out any excess water. Whisk the bloomed gelatine into the hot rum until the gelatine is dissolved. Slowly whisk in the butter in four additions, making sure the butter is completely incorporated before adding more. Slowly stream the mixture into the sweet potato purée, whisking constantly.

5. With a rubber spatula, fold one-third of the whipped cream into the sweet potato base. When fully incorporated, fold in the remaining whipped cream as gently as possible to retain its volume. When finished, the mousse should be uniform in colour, with no streaks of cream, and able to hold a soft peak.

6. Using a rubber spatula, place 2 large scoops of mousse in a piping bag so that it is one-third full. Push the mousse down toward the tip of the bag. Reserve in the refrigerator until needed.

MAKE CHANTILLY CREAM

Make vanilla Chantilly cream, page 185. Using a rubber spatula, place 2 large scoops of Chantilly cream in a piping bag so that it is one-third full. Push the cream down toward the tip of the bag. Refrigerate until needed.

BEGIN ASSEMBLY

1. Line a baking tray with baking paper and place a cone mould on it. Cut an opening about ½ inch (1.25 cm) wide straight across the tip of the piping bag filled with sweet potato mousse. Place the tip of the bag at the bottom of the mould and fill it two-thirds of the way to the top. Using a small offset spatula, spread the mousse up the sides of the mould. This way, you create a space in the centre of the mousse. (You are also eliminating any air pockets that might have formed while piping.) The mousse should measure about ⅜ inch (1 cm) around the sides of the mould.

2. Spoon about 1 teaspoon of citrus marmalade into the space in the centre of the mousse. Gently push a meringue button, flat side up, into the citrus marmalade. To avoid creating air pockets, make sure the button is in full contact with the marmalade.

3. Cut an opening about ⅜ inch (1 cm) wide straight across the tip of the piping bag filled with Chantilly cream. Pipe the cream over the meringue button, making sure to completely cover the entire surface of the meringue. There should be about ⅜ inch (1 cm) left at the top of the mould. Pipe the remaining sweet potato mousse over the cream, filling

the mould. Use a small offset spatula to level off the mousse. Assemble the remaining Mont Blancs in the same fashion. Cover the moulds loosely with plastic wrap and freeze overnight. Reserve the remaining Chantilly cream.

BAKE SABLÉ COOKIES

1. Place a rack in the centre of the oven and preheat the oven to 350°F (175°C) for conventional or 325°F (160°C) for convection. Line a baking tray with baking paper.

2. Remove the cookie dough from the refrigerator and peel off the top layer of baking paper. Using the ring cutter, cut out 6 circles of dough. Place them on the lined baking tray about 1 inch (3 cm) apart. Bake the sablé cookies on the centre rack for 8 minutes. Rotate the tray 180 degrees and bake for 8 minutes more or until golden brown.

3. When the sablé cookies have reached the desired colour, remove from the oven and place them, still on the bsaking paper, on a flat surface. Using the same ring cutter, trim the edges by pushing the ring cutter down through the warm sablé cookie. Let the sablé cookies, still on the baking paper, cool completely.[§]

FINISH ASSEMBLY

1. When the mousse is completely frozen, remove from the moulds by pushing up from the bottom. Invert each mousse cone so the wide base is the bottom. Place each pyramid on top of a sablé cookie.

2. Use the remaining Chantilly cream to decorate the Mont Blancs. Holding the bag at a 90-degree angle about ½ inch (1.25 cm) above the mousse pyramid, pipe a large dot of Chantilly cream, pulling straight up to make a large teardrop.

3. Transfer the finished Mont Blancs to the refrigerator for 2 to 3 hours before serving.

[§] If the baked sablé cookies cool down too much, they will become difficult to cut cleanly. You can always return them to the oven for a minute until they become easier to cut. Just be careful not to overbake them.

SERVING INSTRUCTIONS Let the Mont Blancs sit out for 5 minutes to temper before serving. A light dusting of icing sugar would be a nice touch.

STORAGE INSTRUCTIONS Mont Blancs should be consumed within 24 hours of thawing. They can be kept frozen for up to 1 week without the sablé cookie base (which should be baked the day of).

GINGERBREAD PINECONE

I love making this recipe . . . stacked up beautifully on a multitiered stand to look like a tree for the festive holiday season.

SKILL LEVEL Advanced

TIME 2 hours 30 minutes two days before; 3 hours one day before; 1 hour 30 minutes the day of

YIELD 10 to 12 pinecones

INGREDIENTS

GINGER CREAM

Gelatine sheet (160 bloom)*	2 each	2 each
Pouring cream *(35% milk fat)*	¾ cup, plus more as needed	185 grams, plus more as needed
Chopped peeled fresh ginger	¼ cup	38 grams
Egg yolks (large)	2 each	40 grams
Granulated sugar	2 tablespoons + 1 teaspoon	30 grams

CINNAMON GANACHE

Gelatine sheet (160 bloom)*	½ each	½ each

* If you can't find gelatine sheets, use powdered gelatine.
  One gelatine sheet = 1 scant teaspoon (2.3 grams) powdered gelatine.
  For every teaspoon of gelatine, bloom in 1 tablespoon (15 grams) water.

TIMELINE

TWO DAYS BEFORE Make cream, cinnamon ganache, praliné feuilletine and pear-nutmeg biscuit

ONE DAY BEFORE Whip cream and cinnamon ganache; cut praliné feuilletine; begin assembly; make chocolate décor

THE DAY OF Make chocolate ganache; finish assembly

SPECIAL TOOLS

Medium sieve

Instant-read thermometer

Offset spatula

1¼-inch (3 cm) ring cutter

2 uncut piping bags

2 Ateco #804 plain tips (⅜-inch/ 1 cm diameter)

White chocolate chips	¼ cup	45 grams
Ground cinnamon	½ teaspoon	1.5 grams
Pouring cream *(35% milk fat)*	¾ cup + 2 tablespoons	203 grams

PRALINÉ FEUILLETINE

Milk chocolate *(36% cocoa content)*, finely chopped	3 tablespoon	15 grams
Unsalted butter *(84% butterfat)*	1 teaspoon	4 grams
Feuilletine±	¼ cup	20 grams
Hazelnut paste‡	2 tablespoons	35 grams

PEAR-NUTMEG BISCUIT

Unsalted butter *(84% butterfat)*	3 tablespoons + 1 teaspoon	47 grams
Plain flour	¾ cup	73 grams
Granulated sugar	½ cup	103 grams
Bicarbonate of soda	¼ teaspoon	1 gram
Ground nutmeg	¾ teaspoon	1.75 grams
Kosher salt	½ teaspoon	1 gram
Baking powder	¼ teaspoon	1.5 grams
Whole egg (large; beat 1 egg and measure out half)	½ each	½ each (25 grams)
Pear purée§	⅓ cup + 1 tablespoon	84 grams

CHOCOLATE DÉCOR

Dark chocolate, finely chopped	2 cups	300 grams

DARK CHOCOLATE GANACHE

Water	2 tablespoons	26 grams
Unsweetened cocoa powder	2¼ teaspoons	5 grams
Pouring cream *(35% milk fat)*	¼ cup	57 grams
Whole milk	2 tablespoons	29 grams
Egg yolks (large; beat 2 yolks and measure out three-quarters)	1½ tablespoons	1½ each (30 grams)
Granulated sugar	2 tablespoons	26 grams
Dark chocolate *(66% cocoa content)*, finely chopped	½ cup	83 grams
Icing sugar *(for decoration)*	as needed	as needed

Stand mixer with whisk attachment

2 palette knives

2 acetate sheets, each 15¾ by 11¾ inches (40 by 30 cm)

2 petal or teardrop cutters: ¾-inch (2 cm) and 1-inch (2.5 cm)

± If you can't find feuilletine, you can use any kind of crispy wafers or cookies.

‡ If you can't find hazelnut paste, almond butter is a good substitute.

§ If you can't find pear purée, purée peeled and cored fresh ripe pears, adding 10 per cent of their weight in sugar.

TWO DAYS BEFORE

MAKE CREAM

1. Soak the gelatine sheets in a bowl of ice water until soft, about 20 minutes.* If using powdered gelatine, sprinkle 2 teaspoons (5 grams) gelatine over 2 tablespoons (30 grams) water in a small bowl, stir, and let sit 20 minutes to bloom.

2. Bring the cream to a boil in a small saucepan over medium heat. Remove from the heat and add the ginger. Cover the saucepan with plastic wrap and set it aside to infuse for 20 minutes.

3. Strain the infused cream through a medium sieve into a measuring cup. Add more pouring cream to return it to the original amount. Return the cream to the small saucepan and bring to a boil again over medium heat. Remove from the heat.

4. Whisk the yolks and sugar together in a heatproof bowl. Stream one-third of the hot cream into the yolks, whisking constantly until fully blended, to temper them. Whisk the tempered yolks into the remaining hot cream and return the saucepan to medium heat. Whisking constantly, cook the ginger cream until it reaches 185°F (85°C), begins to bubble slightly and becomes thick. Remove from the heat.

5. If using gelatine sheets, squeeze out any excess water. Whisk the bloomed gelatine into the ginger cream until fully dissolved. Strain the ginger cream through a small sieve into a clean bowl. Cover with plastic wrap pressed directly onto the surface of the cream, to prevent a skin from forming. Refrigerate overnight to set.

MAKE CINNAMON GANACHE

1. Soak the gelatine sheet in a bowl of ice water until soft, about 20 minutes. If using powdered gelatine, sprinkle ½ teaspoon (about 1.5 grams) gelatine over 1½ teaspoons (7.5 grams) ice water in a small bowl, stir, and let sit 20 minutes to bloom.

2. Combine the white chocolate chips and ground cinnamon in a small heatproof bowl.

3. Bring the pouring cream to a boil in a small saucepan over medium heat. Remove from the heat. If using a gelatine sheet, squeeze out any excess water. Whisk the bloomed gelatine into the hot cream until the gelatine is dissolved.

4. Pour the hot cream over the white chocolate and let stand for 30 seconds.

5. Whisk the cream, white chocolate and cinnamon until homogeneous and smooth. Cover with plastic wrap pressed directly onto the surface of the ganache, to prevent a skin from forming. Refrigerate overnight to set.

* Gelatine needs at least 12 hours to set completely. Make sure to plan ahead when using any products that contain gelatine, as they will need time to set.

1. Melt the milk chocolate in a small bowl in the microwave on high power in 20-second intervals, stirring with a heatproof spatula between intervals, until smooth.

2. Melt the butter in the microwave in a medium bowl. Using the spatula, stir in the melted chocolate. Add the feuilletine and hazelnut paste and stir with the spatula until the feuilletine is evenly coated.

3. Spread the feuilletine on a sheet of baking paper, place a second sheet of baking paper on top, and press down. With a rolling pin, roll the feuilletine to a thickness of ¼ inch (5 mm). Transfer the feuilletine, still between the baking paper sheets, to a baking tray and freeze.

MAKE PEAR-NUTMEG BISCUIT

1. Place a rack in the centre of the oven and preheat the oven to 375°F (190°C) for conventional or 350°F (175°C) for convection. Line a quarter baking tray with baking paper.

2. Melt the butter in a small saucepan over medium heat. Remove from the heat and keep warm.

3. Whisk the flour, granulated sugar, bicarbonate of soda, nutmeg, salt and baking powder together in a medium bowl. In another medium bowl, whisk together the egg and pear purée and stream into the dry ingredients, whisking to combine. Continue to whisk until smooth. Slowly stream the melted butter into the batter while whisking. When the butter is completely incorporated, you should have a loose, shiny batter that spreads easily.

4. Using a rubber spatula, scoop the batter onto the quarter baking tray. With an offset spatula, spread the batter evenly to fill the tray so that it is about ¼ inch (6 mm) thick.

5. Bake the biscuit on the centre rack of the oven for 8 minutes. Rotate the tray 180 degrees and bake for 8 minutes more. When finished, the biscuit will be a deep golden brown and spring back to the touch. Let the biscuit, still in the tray, cool completely.

6. Invert the baking tray onto a cutting board. Lift off the tray and peel away the baking paper from the biscuit. Punch out 12 circles of biscuit with a 1¼-inch (3 cm) ring cutter. Wrap with plastic wrap and refrigerate until needed.

ONE DAY BEFORE
WHIP CREAM

Using a whisk, work the ginger cream into a smooth paste. Cut the tip of a piping bag to snugly fit a #804 plain tip. Using a rubber spatula, place 2 large scoops of ginger cream in the bag so that it is one-third full. Push the cream down toward the tip of the bag. Set aside.

WHIP CINNAMON GANACHE

1. Transfer the ganache to a stand mixer fitted with a whisk. Whip on high speed until stiff peaks form.
2. Cut the tip of another piping bag to snugly fit a #804 plain tip. Using a rubber spatula, place 2 large scoops of ganache in the bag so that it is one-third full. Push the ganache down toward the tip of the bag.

CUT PRALINÉ FEUILLETINE

Remove the feuilletine from the freezer. Peel off the top sheet of baking paper. Punch out 12 circles with the 1¼-inch (3 cm) ring cutter. Return to the freezer until needed.

BEGIN ASSEMBLY

1. Line a baking tray with baking paper. Place a praliné feuilletine circle on the pan. On top of that, place a circle of pear-nutmeg biscuit. Make sure to centre the biscuit so that it lines up perfectly with the praliné feuilletine.
2. Holding the piping bag of ginger cream at a 90-degree angle about ½ inch (1.25 cm) above the biscuit, pipe a dot that covers the surface of the biscuit. Use your free hand to hold the biscuit in place. When the cream reaches the edges of the biscuit, pull straight up to create a teardrop shape.
3. Holding the piping bag of cinnamon ganache at a 90-degree angle, start at the base of the biscuit and pipe ganache over the ginger cream, wrapping around the cream and working until it is completely covered. At this point the pinecone will look like it has been wrapped in rope. Repeat with the remaining feuilletine and biscuit circles. Freeze overnight.

MAKE CHOCOLATE DÉCOR

1. Melt and temper the dark chocolate (see page 242).
2. Place a sheet of baking paper on the work surface. Using a palette knife, on the first sheet of acetate spread half of the tempered chocolate in a thin, even layer about the thickness of a credit card. When the chocolate is no longer shiny, use the large petal cutter to punch out 250 chocolate pieces. You will have just 2 to 3 minutes before the chocolate is fully set, so speed is very important. When you are done, flip the sheet over onto the baking paper so the acetate is facing up. This will keep the chocolate flat as it sets.
3. Repeat the process using the small petal cutter on the second sheet of acetate and cut 250 petals. When finished, place it on top of the first sheet and let them both set in the refrigerator for 20 minutes.

4. Peel off the acetate and separate the chocolate décor. Store in an airtight container at room temperature.

THE DAY OF

MAKE CHOCOLATE GANACHE

1. Whisk the water and cocoa powder in a small bowl to make a smooth paste. Set aside at room temperature.
2. Combine the cream and milk in a small saucepan and bring to a boil over medium heat. Remove from the heat. Whisk the egg yolks and granulated sugar in a small bowl until fully blended.±
3. Stream one-third of the hot cream and milk into the egg yolks, whisking constantly until fully blended, to temper them. Whisk the tempered yolks into the remaining hot cream and milk and return the saucepan to medium heat.
4. Continue to cook the custard over medium heat, whisking continuously, until it reaches 185°F (85°C). The custard will turn pale yellow and thicken so that it coats the back of a spoon. Remove from the heat, add the cocoa powder paste, and whisk until fully blended.
5. Place the dark chocolate in a heatproof bowl. Strain the custard through a small sieve over the chocolate. Let stand for 30 seconds.
6. Whisk the chocolate and custard until homogeneous and smooth. When finished, the ganache will have the consistency of pancake batter and be pourable.

FINISH ASSEMBLY

1. Line a baking tray with baking paper and place a wire rack on top. Take the pinecone bases out of the freezer and arrange them on the wire rack, about 3 inches (7.5 cm) apart.
2. Make sure the dark chocolate ganache is between 95° and 104°F (35° and 40°C), or slightly warm to the touch. Let it cool further or rewarm it gently over simmering water if necessary.‡
3. Pour the chocolate ganache directly over the top of a frozen pinecone so that it covers the entire structure. Repeat with the remaining pinecones. Refrigerate for 5 minutes to set lightly.
4. With an offset spatula, transfer the pinecones from the wire rack to a baking tray or individual serving plates. Let thaw in the refrigerator for 2 to 3 hours before applying the décor.
5. Starting at the bottom of the pinecone, and with the smaller petals first, place the pointed end of the décor into the ganache, rounded end facing up. Place the next piece of décor directly next to the first one. Repeat until the décor completely wraps around the pinecone. Make a

± Combine the sugar and egg yolks just before using. Over time, the sugar will 'cook' the egg yolks, creating lumps.

‡ At this temperature, the chocolate ganache is fluid enough to coat the pinecone without melting the cinnamon ganache underneath.

second row ½ inch (1.25 cm) above the first. Complete a third and final row of small petals.

6. Toward the centre, start using the larger petals and then switch to the smaller petals again at the top.

7. Continue to fill the pinecone with décor until you reach the top (a minimum of 6 layers and up to 12 layers of décor total). A finished pinecone will use around 40 pieces of chocolate décor. Continue with the remaining pinecones.[§] Keep in the refrigerator until ready to serve.

§ As you reach the top 3 layers of décor, start to angle the petals up to more closely resemble a pinecone.

SERVING INSTRUCTIONS Let the pinecones sit out for 5 minutes to temper before serving. Immediately before serving, sift icing sugar over the pinecones to give the appearance of snow.

STORAGE INSTRUCTIONS Consume within 24 hours of glazing. Unglazed pinecones can be kept frozen for up to 1 week. The décor can be kept in a closed airtight container at room temperature for up to 1 week.

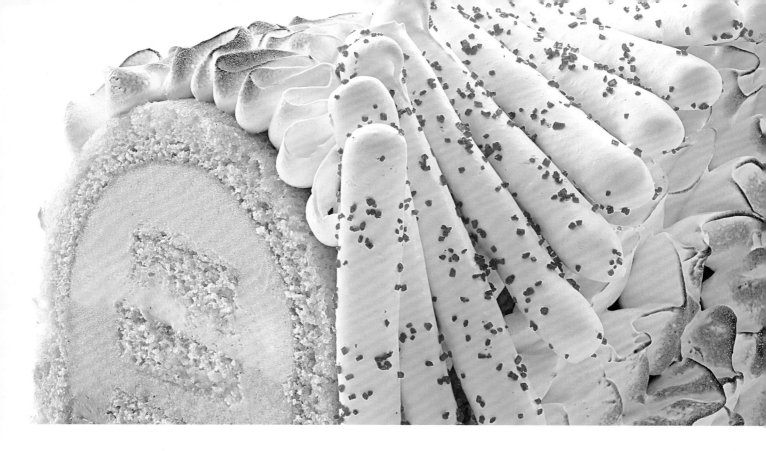

BAKED ALASKA

I love making this recipe . . . for large parties that require a 'wow' factor.

SKILL LEVEL Advanced

TIME 2 hours 30 minutes two days before; 3 hours 30 minutes one day before; 2 hours the day of

YIELD 1 large cake to serve 8 to 10 people

INGREDIENTS

Almond biscuit (page 141)	2 batches	2 batches
Vanilla Ice Cream base (page 124); chilled but not churned	1 batch	1 batch

SMOKED CINNAMON ICE CREAM

Whole milk	2⅓ cups	548 grams
Pouring cream *(35% milk fat)*	¼ cup + 1 tablespoon	61 grams
Ground cinnamon, preferably smoked	1¼ teaspoons	3 grams
Granulated sugar	½ cup + 1 tablespoon	116 grams
Milk powder	⅓ cup	30 g
Egg yolks (large), at room temperature	5 each	5 each (100 grams)
Unsalted butter *(84% butterfat)*	3 tablespoons	42 grams

TIMELINE

TWO DAYS BEFORE Make biscuit, ice creams and sorbet bases

ONE DAY BEFORE Make caramelized sablé cookie crumbs and Calvados syrup; begin assembly

THE DAY OF Make meringues; finish assembly

SPECIAL TOOLS

Instant-read thermometer

Small sieve

Smoking gun (optional)

Apple wood chips (optional)

Stand mixer with paddle and whisk attachments

Pastry brush

10 by 4 by 4–inch (25 by 10 by 10 cm) terrine mold

Ice cream machine

6 uncut piping bags

CARAMEL ICE CREAM

Granulated sugar	¾ cup	154 grams
Unsalted butter *(84% butterfat)*	2½ tablespoons	35 grams
Whole milk	2¼ cups	528 grams
Pouring cream *(35% milk fat)*	¼ cup + 1 teaspoon	59 grams
Milk powder	⅓ cup + 1 tablespoon	30 grams
Kosher salt	1 teaspoon	2 grams
Egg yolks (large), at room temperature	5 each	5 each (100 grams)

GREEN APPLE SORBET

Water	1¼ cups + 2½ tablespoons	263 grams
Granulated sugar	¾ cup	154 grams
Green apple purée	2½ cups	566 grams
Calvados	1 tablespoon + 1 teaspoon	15 grams

CARAMELISED SABLÉ BRETON COOKIE CRUMBS

Sablé Breton cookie dough (page 126), unbaked	1 batch	1 batch
Light corn syrup	2 tablespoons	37 grams
Glazing fondant	2 tablespoons	37 grams

CALVADOS SYRUP

Granulated sugar	¼ cup	50 grams
Water	½ cup + 1 tablespoon	115 grams
Calvados	¼ cup + 1 tablespoon	75 grams
Swiss meringue (page 116)	1 batch	1 batch
Red sanding sugar *(for decoration)*	2 tablespoons	16 grams

Ateco #804 plain tip (⅜-inch/ 1 cm diameter)

Rose tip (½-inch/1.25 cm wide)

Blowtorch

TWO DAYS BEFORE

MAKE BISCUIT

Bake a double batch of the almond biscuit in the Cotton-Soft Cheesecake recipe, page 141. It can be baked without cutting. Let cool to room temperature, then wrap well in plastic wrap and refrigerate.

MAKE VANILLA ICE CREAM BASE

Prepare the base for vanilla ice cream but do not churn it yet. Strain it through a small sieve into a 1 litre container. Fill a large bowl with ice and water. Place the container of ice cream base in the ice bath. Stir the base with a whisk every 10 minutes to cool it rapidly. When fully cooled, refrigerate until needed.[*]

* Since you will pipe the ice cream, you want to churn it right before you assemble the baked Alaska.

MAKE (SMOKED) CINNAMON ICE CREAM BASE

1. For extra flavour, place the ground cinnamon in a resealable plastic bag. Fit the tip of the smoking gun filled with apple wood chips into the bag and seal. Let the smoke fill the bag and close. Set aside for 30 minutes, so the ground cinnamon can absorb the smoke.

2. Combine the milk, cream and (smoked) cinnamon in a medium saucepan and warm over low heat. Whisk the granulated sugar and milk powder together in a medium bowl. Whisk into the milk mixture, raise the heat to medium and bring to a boil. When the sugar and milk powder have dissolved, remove from the heat.

3. Place the egg yolks in a medium heatproof bowl and whisk them to blend lightly. Stream one-third of the hot milk mixture into the yolks, whisking constantly until fully blended, to temper them. Whisk the tempered yolks into the remaining hot milk and return the saucepan to medium heat.

4. Continue to cook the base over medium heat, whisking continuously, until it reaches 185°F (85°C) and becomes thick enough to coat the back of a spoon. Add the butter and whisk until melted. Remove from the heat. Strain through a small sieve into a 1 litre container.

5. Fill a large bowl with ice and water. Place the container of ice cream base in the ice bath. Stir the base with a whisk every 10 minutes to cool it rapidly. When fully cooled, refrigerate until needed.

MAKE CARAMEL ICE CREAM BASE

1. Place a medium saucepan over high heat. Sprinkle about one-quarter of the granulated sugar into the hot pan. As the sugar melts and starts to caramelise, stir with a heatproof spatula until all the sugar crystals dissolve. Slowly sprinkle in the remaining sugar, stirring as you sprinkle. When all the sugar has been added, continue to cook until the colour reaches a deep amber. Whisk in the butter until completely incorporated.

2. Combine the whole milk and pouring cream in another medium saucepan. Bring to a boil over medium heat. Remove from the heat.

3. Pour the caramel onto a quarter baking tray lined with baking paper. Cool at room temperature for 30 minutes. Once cool, break the sheeted caramel into small pieces. Add to the warm milk mixture and cover with plastic wrap to infuse, about 30 minutes.

4. Remove the plastic wrap from the caramel-infused milk and whisk in the milk powder and salt.

5. Place the egg yolks in a small heatproof bowl and whisk them to blend lightly. Stream in one-third of the caramel-infused milk, whisking until fully blended, to temper the yolks. Whisk the tempered yolks into the remaining caramel-infused milk and return the saucepan to medium heat. Continue to cook the base over medium heat, whisking continuously, until it reaches 185°F (85°C) and becomes thick enough to

coat the back of a spoon. Remove from the heat. Strain through a small sieve into a 1 litre container.

6. Fill a large bowl with ice and water. Place the container of ice cream base in the ice bath. Stir the base with a whisk every 10 minutes to cool it rapidly. When fully cooled, refrigerate until needed.

MAKE GREEN APPLE SORBET BASE

1. Combine the water and granulated sugar in a medium saucepan over medium heat. Bring to a boil and cook until the sugar is dissolved. Remove from the heat and let cool for a few minutes.

2. Whisk in the green apple purée and Calvados until fully blended. Transfer to a 1 litre container and set aside to cool to room temperature. When cooled, refrigerate until needed.

ONE DAY BEFORE

MAKE CARAMELISED SABLÉ COOKIE CRUMBS

1. Bake and cool the sablé Breton cookie dough recipe, page 126. It can be baked without cutting. Place the baked sablé in a stand mixer fitted with a paddle. Mix on low speed until the sablé turns into sandy crumbs.

2. Combine the corn syrup and glazing fondant in a small saucepan. Bring the syrup to a boil over medium heat and continue to cook until the caramel turns a deep amber colour.

3. Increase the mixer speed to medium and slowly pour the caramel down the sides of the bowl, being careful to avoid the paddle. When all the caramel has been added, continue to beat the sablé cookie crumbs for 20 seconds more so that the caramel is evenly distributed.

4. Pour the caramelised sablé cookie crumbs onto a baking tray lined with baking paper and let cool completely. When cooled, reserve in an airtight container.

MAKE CALVADOS SYRUP

Combine the granulated sugar and water in a small saucepan. Bring to a boil over medium heat. Remove from the heat and let the syrup cool to room temperature. Whisk the Calvados into the syrup. Reserve at room temperature until needed.

BEGIN ASSEMBLY

1. Remove the plastic wrap from the almond biscuit and place skin side down on a baking tray lined with baking paper. With a pastry brush, apply the Calvados syrup.

2. Line the terrine mould lengthwise with a 14 by 4–inch (40 by 10 cm) strip of baking paper, leaving a 1-inch (2.5 cm) overhang at each end.

3. Cut the almond biscuit the same size as the baking paper, letting the

biscuit come 1 inch (2.5 cm) above the edge of the mould just like the baking paper. Cut three 1½ by 10–inch (3 by 25 cm) strips of biscuit and reserve until needed. These will be layered between each of the ice cream flavours.

4. Churn the vanilla ice cream according to the instructions for your machine.

5. Using a rubber spatula, place 2 large scoops of the vanilla ice cream in a piping bag so that it is one-third full. Cut an opening about 1 inch (2.5 cm) wide straight across the tip of the bag. Pipe a layer of ice cream about ¾ inch (2 cm) thick into the bottom of the mould. Push one of the strips of almond biscuit into the ice cream, forcing the ice cream to the sides of the mould and creating a level layer. Apply the Calvados syrup to the biscuit liberally. Reserve in the freezer.

6. Churn the (smoked) cinnamon ice cream. Transfer to another piping bag. Cut an opening about 1 inch (2.5 cm) wide straight across the tip of the bag. Pipe a layer of (smoked) cinnamon ice cream about ¾ inch (2 cm) thick on top of the biscuit in the mould. Push a second strip of almond biscuit into the (smoked) cinnamon ice cream, forcing the ice cream to the sides of the mould and creating a level layer. Return the mould to the freezer.

7. Churn the caramel ice cream. Transfer it to a third piping bag. Cut an opening about 1 inch (2.5 cm) wide straight across the tip of the bag. Pipe a layer of caramel ice cream about ¾ inch (2 cm) thick on top of the biscuit in the mould. Push the last strip of almond biscuit into the caramel ice cream, forcing the ice cream to the sides of the mould and creating a level layer. Return the mould to the freezer.

8. Finally, churn the green apple sorbet. Transfer it to a fourth piping bag. Cut an opening about 1 inch (2.5 cm) wide straight across the tip of the bag. Pipe a layer of sorbet about ¾ inch (2 cm) thick into the mould.

9. Cover the green apple sorbet with half the caramelised sablé cookie crumbs. Gently push the crumbs into the sorbet so that they will stick when the baked Alaska is unmoulded. Reserve the rest of the crumbs. Cover the mould with plastic wrap and freeze the baked Alaska overnight.

THE DAY OF

MAKE MERINGUES

1. Make Swiss meringue, page 116.

2. Preheat the oven to 200°F (95°C) for conventional or 175°F (80°C) for convection.

3. Cut the tip of a piping bag to snugly fit a #804 plain tip. Using a rubber spatula, place 2 large scoops of Swiss meringue in the bag so that it is one-third full. Push the meringue down toward the tip of the bag.

4. Line a half baking tray with baking paper. At each corner, pipe a small

dot of meringue under the baking paper and push the paper flat. This will help keep it 'glued' to the baking tray.

5. Holding the piping bag at a 45-degree angle about ½ inch (1.25 cm) above the baking tray, with steady, even pressure pipe sticks of meringue about 3 inches (7.5 cm) long. When you reach the end of a stick, quickly pull the tip straight up. Pipe sticks about 1 inch (2.5 cm) apart until you have at least 40 meringue sticks. Sprinkle with red sanding sugar. Refrigerate the remaining Swiss meringue until needed to decorate the baked Alaska.

6. Bake the meringue sticks for 20 minutes. Rotate the tray 180 degrees and bake for 20 minutes more. Continue to rotate every 20 minutes until the meringue sticks are completely dry, about 1 hour 20 minutes.

7. Let the meringue sticks, still on the baking paper, cool completely. When cool, remove gently from the paper with your fingers. Reserve in an airtight container until needed.

FINISH ASSEMBLY

1. Slide a hot knife around each side of the terrine. Gently pull the baking paper to unmould the baked Alaska.

2. Cut the tip of a piping bag to snugly fit a ½-inch (1.25 cm) rose tip. Using a rubber spatula, place 2 large scoops of the reserved meringue in the bag so that it is one-third full. Push the meringue down toward the tip of the bag.

3. Using the meringue in the piping bag, slowly place the meringue sticks vertically over the baked Alaska in a wave, starting at the bottom right and ending in the opposite corner. This should take about 30 meringue sticks.

4. Pipe the Swiss meringue around the uncovered areas of the baked Alaska. Starting at the bottom corner, pipe horizontally across the baked Alaska, moving the tip back and forth about 1 inch (2.5 cm) to form undulating waves.±

5. Coat the two exposed ends of the baked Alaska with the remaining caramelised sablé cookie crumbs, firmly pushing the crumbs into the ice cream and sorbet.

6. Hold the tip of the blowtorch about 3 inches (7.5 cm) from the meringue and lightly toast the outside of the baked Alaska.

± There are other ways to decorate the baked Alaska. One alternative is to use a #804 plain tip and pipe teardrops to cover the almond biscuit, giving you a spiked appearance. Another is to spread the meringue with your hands, creating a natural wavy texture.

SERVING INSTRUCTIONS Let temper 5 minutes before cutting and serving.

STORAGE INSTRUCTIONS The undecorated baked Alaska can be frozen for up to 1 week before serving. Meringue sticks can be stored in a closed airtight container for up to 1 week.

ADDITIONAL
TECHNIQUES

COOKING CUSTARD

Any cream base that contains eggs is considered a custard. You'll find it in ice cream bases, pastry cream, crème anglaise, some ganaches and all sorts of baked flans. Curds are made in a similar fashion.

Eggs can be tricky to cook because they are so temperature sensitive. Any temperature higher than 185°F (85°C) and you'll get scrambled eggs. When in doubt, always follow these two quick tips:

1. Temper the eggs by slowly streaming in one-third of the hot liquid, whisking constantly. This will raise the temperature of the eggs just enough so that you can return them to the rest of the hot liquid without overheating and instantly cooking them. This way, you'll get a silky texture.

2. When the eggs return to the hot mixture, they are not quite cooked through yet. You will need to keep whisking until the custard reaches a state called *nappé*, which means 'glazed' in French and refers to when the custard is thick enough to coat the back of a spoon. Draw a line with your finger through the coated portion of the spoon. You should get a clear line, as the liquid won't flow through.

When refrigerating custard, always place plastic wrap directly on the surface to prevent a skin from forming.

PÂTE À CHOUX

Pâte à choux is one of my favourite doughs to work with because I can create so many shapes with this combination of milk, butter, salt, sugar, flour and eggs—from the long fingers of éclairs to the circular rings of the Paris-Brest. But perhaps the most common form it takes is a small circular puff, from which it got its name—*choux* means 'cabbage' in French—and it's also the sweet name that my mum calls my dad at home.

BASIC STEPS FOR PÂTE À CHOUX

1. Boil the milk, butter, salt and sugar.
2. Add the flour and use some elbow grease to mix the dough vigorously with a wooden spoon until it starts to dry and form a skin on the bottom of the saucepan. This is referred to in French as *desséché*, meaning 'dehydrated'. (It's important to let some of the water evaporate so that you can add eggs to the dough without making it too runny.)
3. Transfer the dough to a bowl and beat to cool slightly. Beat in the eggs one by one. (You can also use a stand mixer.)
4. When the dough is done, you should be able to lift the spoon and draw out a ribbon that slowly dissolves into the dough after a few seconds.

HERE'S A TRICK: Usually pâte à choux is made and used right away. But a few years ago, someone at the bakery mistakenly left it in the refrigerator overnight. When we tried to use it the next day, the results were even better than usual. The pâte à choux didn't puff up as much and maintained its shape more cleanly as it baked.

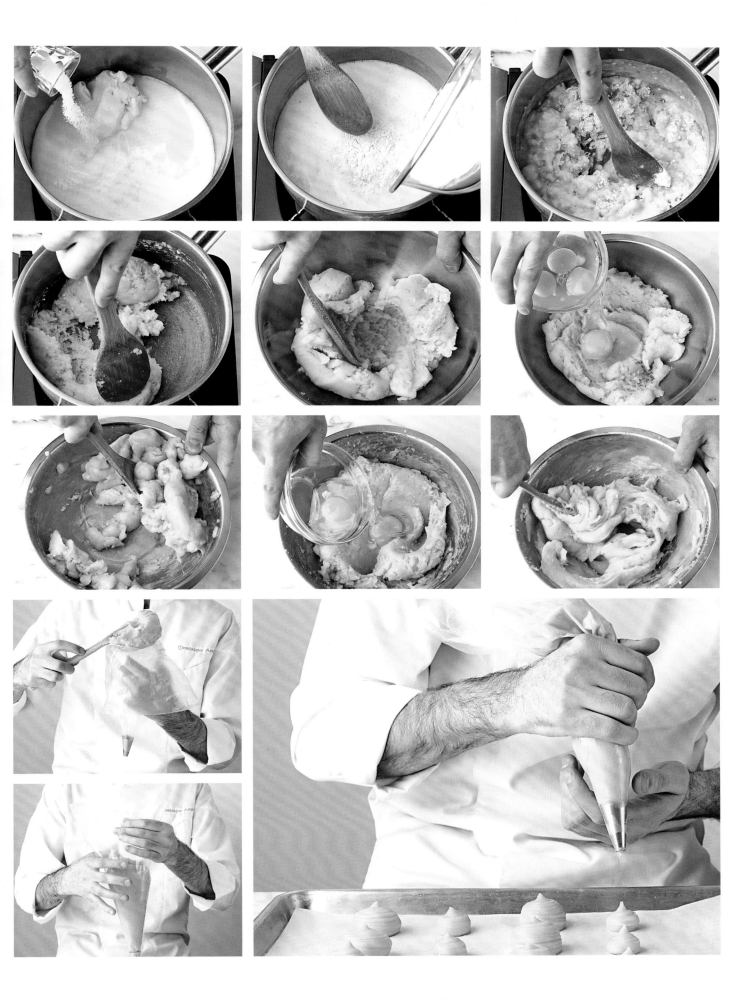

PIPING

I'm the first to admit that I don't have great handwriting, but when I pipe the letters with a cornet, they turn out pretty well. In culinary school, we practised how to properly pipe by writing the alphabet in Gothic script every day for weeks.

Piping well is something that takes a lot of repetition. Don't give up—it takes time to develop the right kind of accuracy and consistency needed to pipe.

TIPS ON PIPING

1. The open top of the piping bag should always be folded over your hand so that you can fill it without getting the top part of the bag dirty.
2. If you're using a tip, always make sure the tip fits snugly into the bottom of the bag before filling it.
3. Don't overfill the bag. You'll have more control when your hand is closer to the tip.
4. Always twist the open top of the bag to make sure the material you're piping doesn't spill out.
5. Use your free hand to steady the tip while you squeeze with the hand holding the bag.
6. When you are done piping the shape, release the pressure and quickly pull up, turning your wrist slightly at the same time.
7. Piping at a 90-degree angle always gives you better control and a more even shape.
8. If you aren't very confident when it comes to piping freehand, you can make guide marks on the piece of baking paper you're piping onto. Just remember to turn the paper over so that the ink or pencil is on the reverse side.

TEMPERING CHOCOLATE

One of the most important skills for a pastry cook to develop when advancing is how to temper chocolate. When melted, the cocoa butter in chocolate doesn't naturally resolidify into the proper crystallisation structure. The goal of tempering is simple: to form the right types of crystallisation in the cocoa butter so that you get chocolate that has a shiny surface and snaps cleanly when broken. Untempered chocolate sets matte, often with white streaks of cocoa butter on the surface (this is called 'bloom') and crumbles rather than breaks evenly.

When I first started to learn how to temper chocolate, I practised on my kitchen table at home. Chocolate was everywhere, but that may be the type of spirit you need to learn this essential pastry skill. Throw yourself into the challenge.

There are two techniques for tempering:

TABLETOP TECHNIQUE FOR TEMPERING

1. Start with a marble or granite surface, which is clean and dry and doesn't absorb the heat.
2. Melt the chocolate to the proper temperature.
   Dark chocolate: 118°F (48°C)
   Milk chocolate: 113°F (45°C)
   White chocolate: 109°F (43°C)
3. Pour 80 per cent of the melted chocolate onto the work space. Using two palette knives, slowly move the chocolate around to agitate it. Scrape the knives against each other to clean them as you work.
4. Watch as the chocolate starts to thicken and develop a gleam. The temperature should be about 84°F (29°C), and the chocolate should feel slightly cool to the touch, as it's just below body temperature.
5. Return the agitated chocolate to the bowl with the remaining melted chocolate, using the palette knives. The agitated chocolate will reheat slightly as the whole amount comes to the proper temperature.
   Dark chocolate: 88°F (31°C)
   Milk chocolate: 86°F (30°C)
   White chocolate: 86°F (30°C)

In your first few times tempering, always make sure to test by dipping an offset spatula or piece of baking paper into the chocolate to see if it sets shiny. If not, try again with the same chocolate. Once tempered, chocolate must be used immediately. If it solidifies, retemper.

SEEDING TECHNIQUE FOR TEMPERING

1. Melt two-thirds of the chocolate that you want to temper.
2. Finely chop the remaining one-third. Slowly mix it into the melted chocolate with a rubber spatula. (This is also referred to as 'agitating the chocolate'.) As you add the chopped chocolate and 'seed' the melted chocolate, it will cool. (Think of it like adding ice cubes to a sink full of water.)
3. The chocolate should be tempered when all the chopped chocolate has been incorporated.

This technique may be faster, but it's less precise. It is a great alternative for smaller kitchens.

FIRE AND WATER

Two things will ruin chocolate and make it un-usable:

1. If you heat chocolate on its own to over 129°F (54°C), you will burn or scorch it.
2. If you wet the chocolate with water or steam while tempering it, the chocolate will seize and turn grainy and pasty.

LAMINATION

Lamination is a technique of layering dough with butter. It is responsible for the flaky texture of many of our favourite French pastry classics such as the croissant, and Danish and puff pastry.

When I was going through my training, laminated doughs were always one of the last things on the curriculum because they required fast hands and a large time commitment; the dough needs to rest while being layered. It can take up to 3 days to laminate some doughs.

BASIC STEPS TO LAMINATION
1. There are always two parts: the dough and the butter block. Both need to be chilled after mixing and shaping so they are cold and firm but still flexible. It is very important that the butter and dough are similar in temperature, texture and consistency to form even layers.

2. Standard lamination places the butter block within the dough. Inverse lamination (often used for puff pastry because it results in a flakier texture) has the butter on the outside and the dough within. The outer layer is folded up over the inner layer to enclose it completely, then chilled.

3. Now begin the folds. Roll out the dough-and-butter package from top to bottom into a long rectangle. Each time you roll out the dough, the seam side should face up to make sure it doesn't slip and slide as you work the dough with the rolling pin.

4. Depending on what pastry you're making, you will either do a letter fold (which is folded in thirds, like a letter going into an envelope) or a book fold (which is folded in half, like a book).

5. Usually, you rest the dough in the refrigerator for at least 30 minutes between folds to ensure the butter doesn't start to warm up and leak out.

ACKNOWLEDGMENTS

A big thank-you to:

My amazing team at the Bakery—and to Noah in particular for his hard work.

The people who supported me throughout the production of this book—
Amy, Emily, Thomas, Sahinaz, Suet, Seth and Mike.

Daniel Boulud (aka Papa).

Simon & Schuster.

And my fans from around the world for their passion and support.

INDEX

Note: Page numbers in *italics* refer to illustrations.